DIFFERENT KINDS OF MINDS

A GUIDE TO YOUR BRAIN

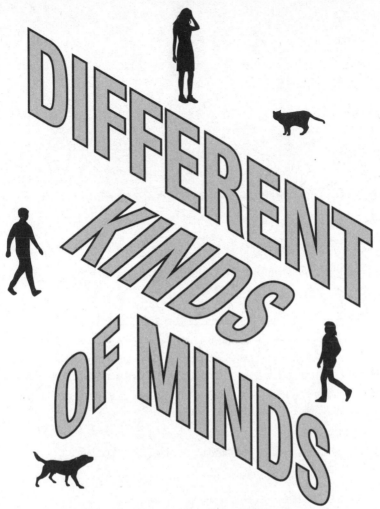

DIFFERENT KINDS OF MINDS

A GUIDE TO YOUR BRAIN

TEMPLE GRANDIN

with ANN D. KOFFSKY

PHILOMEL

PHILOMEL

An imprint of Penguin Random House LLC, New York

First published in the United States of America by Philomel,
an imprint of Penguin Random House LLC, 2023

Copyright © 2023 by Temple Grandin

Image credits on p. 231

Philomel is a registered trademark of Penguin Random House LLC.
The Penguin colophon is a registered trademark of Penguin Books Limited.

Visit us online at PenguinRandomHouse.com.

Library of Congress Cataloging-in-Publication Data is available.

ISBN 9780593352878

1st Printing

Printed in the United States of America

LSCH

Edited by Jill Santopolo

Design by Lucia Baez

Text set in Sabon LT Std

Dedicated to all the
students and people who
think differently

CONTENTS

Introduction

WHAT DO YOU WANT TO BE WHEN YOU GROW UP? It's probably the number one question adults ask kids. I think it's the wrong question. Instead, I like to ask kids: What are you good at? Drawing? Working with your hands? Do you like music, math, writing, computers, fixing things? Sewing? Cooking? Building? Are you good with people? Animals? Do you like to play chess or Scrabble? Are you good at memorizing or do you need to write everything down? Do you like maps, puzzles, and brainteasers? Do you like stories or facts? One more question: Is your room a big mess or do you keep things organized? All these questions have one thing in common. They are clues to how you think, to how your brain works.

When I was growing up, my speech was delayed and I couldn't make eye contact or make friends. The doctor told my parents I was brain damaged. Eventually, I was diagnosed with autism, which is a developmental disorder that affects speech and communication. It can be mild or quite severe. In my case, I had tantrums, no interest in people, and I often stared off into space. Neurotypical children (those who develop in predictable ways) naturally connect language to the things in their lives. Autistic children, however, need to learn that objects have names. I was lucky that my mother taught me how to read when I was eight. With a lot of hard work and tutoring, I was able to finish high school and college and get my PhD in animal science. I still had difficulty fitting in with the social kids, but my best friends shared my interests in horses, model rockets, and building electronic circuits. As I talk about in this book, not fitting in can be a huge benefit, and seeing things differently, or having a brain that processes information in a new way, can lead to innovation, discovery, and invention.

I started to understand these differences when I realized that I didn't think the same way as other people. Most people think in a combination of words and vague, generalized pictures. I am a picture thinker, or visual thinker, 100 percent. My mother noticed my abilities in the second and third grade when I painted watercolors of the beach, and then later when I modeled a clay horse that was almost identical to a real horse. When I hear a word like "dog," my mind clicks through every dog I've seen, like scrolling through photo albums on a phone or looking at Google Images. Later, when I started designing industrial equipment, I could draw an accurate blueprint without ever having taken a drafting class. If I could see the structure in my imagination, I could draw it.

People who are visual thinkers like me tend to be good at art, working with animals, design, architecture, building, and mechanical skills, such as fixing cars. In my quest to understand visual thinking, I discovered that there is another type of visual thinker called spatial visual thinkers. These people are often good at music, math, computer programming, and things that require an ability with abstraction (ideas) and patterns (connections between things). I was always terrible at algebra, and that's a big deal because in most schools, if you can't do algebra, you can't advance to the next level. Studies now show that there is a reason why some people are "bad at math." It's the way their minds work. I'm not saying that math isn't important, but some people who are good at trigonometry and geometry can't do algebra. Instead of making everyone fulfill the same requirements, I believe we need to appreciate the different ways our minds work.

I have observed that kids who are good at writing and test taking and who have neat backpacks and binders tend to have an easier time at school. They have strong organizational skills, and reading and writing are generally easier for them to learn. These kids tend to be verbal thinkers, meaning they think in words. The way schools and testing are set up with an emphasis on reading and writing, these students have an advantage.

In my day, there were lots of hands-on classes like shop (woodworking), art, sewing, music, theater, and so forth. It gave kids who struggled with taking tests a chance to discover what they were good at. For me, it was doing things with my hands, like woodworking and sewing. I made the sets for our school plays and sewed costumes. Later, in boarding school, I fed and took care of the horses, including mucking out the stables. All these experiences paved the way for me as a designer and an animal expert. These skills have something important in common: they require strong visual thinking and are nonverbal activities. This is why I like to ask kids what they are good at. I don't think there is anything more valuable than finding out what you are good at and having opportunities to develop those skills.

I had several experiences that set the course of my life and career. When I visited my aunt's cattle farm, I discovered my love of animals, but I was also obsessed with building and fixing things. One of my inventions was a gate for the driveway that you could open from the car. I also remember when I observed a cattle squeeze chute that calmed the animals when they were vaccinated. It had two panels that pressed their sides. A few days later, when I had a panic attack, I got inside the chute to see if it would calm me. I felt a wave of relaxation and afterward copied the design for the first human squeeze machine. People didn't understand it at first, but now my "Hug Machine" is used all over the world to help people with autism manage their anxiety. Being a visual thinker helped me see the connection between the squeeze chute for the cattle and my own needs. I was also able to build it because of both my ability to visualize it and my familiarity with tools, which I had grown up using. These are not the kinds of skills you will find on the SAT, but they are every bit as important.

You may have heard the famous quote "I think, therefore I am," by René Descartes. He was a seventeenth-century philosopher who believed that what separates us from animals is language. (I guess what he meant was: "I have language, therefore I am.") That theory has never been challenged; we communicate in words, we speak, and animals don't. At least not in human language. But as someone who didn't have speech until I was four, and who primarily thinks in pictures, not words, I made it one of my life's goals to understand different ways of thinking. Without language, Descartes would conclude that I didn't exist. I guess I would say to Descartes, "I think in pictures, therefore I am!"

When it comes to thinking, one size does not fit all. Have you ever wondered why your brother is great at piano and you can't carry a tune, or why one of your parents likes to follow directions to get somewhere and the other wings it? If you've ever given any thought to why you're great at writing but hate math, this book attempts to answer those questions. I also delve into how different minds can work together, as each brings different strengths. I talk about genius and the kinds of minds that have contributed to the world's great advancements and innovations. I explore the types of danger that verbal people might miss. (Visual thinkers are needed to prevent potential disasters caused by engineering mistakes.) I end with a chapter about animals. Until recently, animals were mostly considered non-sentient, or non-feeling, and science warns us not to "anthropomorphize," meaning attach human emotion to animal behavior. But there is still considerable disagreement in the scientific community as to whether animals have emotions, if they can think. Most people with pets probably disagree with Descartes. Animals may not be verbal, but they feel through their senses. They are visual, auditory, and sensory thinkers.

While I was doing research for this book, I had two experiences that were game changers. In 2019, I toured a state-of-the-art poultry-processing plant. This is a component of my job as a consultant in the food supply business. One of my responsibilities is making sure the plants are operating correctly and identifying problems with equipment. I'm known for spotting things that aren't right (another benefit of being a visual thinker). But that day something else jumped out at me. At this plant, the equipment was brand new. It was beautiful, meticulously crafted, and made of gleaming stainless steel with many moving parts. I knew it would take highly skilled, highly paid workers to maintain and repair the equipment. Until then, nearly every plant I had worked at used equipment made in America, but here I discovered that the equipment had been imported from the Netherlands. I had no idea how we would fix it when it broke.

Then I visited the Steve Jobs Theater at Apple's headquarters in Cupertino, California. It looks like a spaceship from another galaxy. The walls are sheer glass, and the electrical, sprinkler, audio, and security systems are hidden in the seams between the glass. I was fascinated by every aspect of it and came to learn that the glass was imported from Germany, the lightweight carbon-fiber roof was from Dubai, and the glass walls of the theater had been engineered in Italy. I stood in the middle of the lobby and cried out, "We don't make it anymore!"

Temple Grandin standing in the lobby of the Steve Jobs Theater, exclaiming, "We don't make it anymore!"

This was just the beginning of my fast-growing realization that our country was losing its ability to produce the equipment we need to stay competitive with the rest of the world. Throughout history, the U.S. had been a leader in ingenuity, innovation, and invention.

What was happening? As schools have focused more on scores and testing, we have been "screening out" the people with visual skills. Imagine a world with no artists, designers, or inventors. No electricians, mechanics, architects, plumbers. I call these people "the clever engineers." They can invent things, fix things, and improve systems. Being "good with your hands" is more than just being handy. It's as if there is an invisible connection between your hands and your brain. It's automatic. Without these clever engineers, we are going to fall behind even more. My goal is to get hands-on education back into schools so that we don't screen out the people we need.

How can you tell if you're a visual thinker? Are you good at art, music, putting mechanical things together? Or would you rather invent stories and keep a diary? These are clues. Are you a master Lego builder—so good, you maybe don't need the instructions? Would you rather write an essay than paint a picture? We all use visual and verbal thinking to navigate the world, or, to put it another way, we are all on a spectrum with extreme skills at either end, and most people fall somewhere in the middle. To be happy and successful at what you do, we need schools and parents and caregivers to encourage you to do the things you're good at. Sometimes these gifts are obvious, and sometimes they are hidden. For me, understanding the way I think has enriched my life and career. I don't want to be like everyone else. I hope this book will help you figure out what kind of thinker you are, what you're good at, and how to use those skills to make the world a better place.

CHAPTER ONE
What Is Visual Thinking?

WHEN I WAS TWO AND A HALF YEARS OLD, MY mother took me to the doctor to find out why I wasn't developing the same way as other children my age. Neighborhood kids were able to socialize and make friends, while I had trouble even making eye contact. Children my age could say simple sentences like "Let's play" or "I'm hungry," while I couldn't say "Mommy" or "Daddy." My parents were concerned; why were my speech and social skills so delayed?

The doctor examined me, and at the end of the visit announced that I was "brain damaged." It was 1949. Doctors hadn't started using the word "autistic" for children like me yet. They thought something was terribly wrong with me.

I was fortunate. My parents made sure that I got speech therapy, and eventually I learned to speak. But it took me many more years to learn what doctors today comprehend: that different people think and learn differently.

What Is Autism?

Autism is referred to as a spectrum disorder, meaning that there is a range of symptoms among people with autism. Being autistic can mean many different things, and it can include everyone from a very capable person who works as an engineer at Apple to another person who needs lots of care and has trouble being on their own. I think it's more correct to describe autism as a behavioral profile instead of a disorder. People with autism often have difficulty with social skills, like making conversation and looking people in the eye. They often learn to speak at older ages and sometimes engage in repetitive behaviors (like opening and closing a door many times in a row). According to the Centers for Disease Control and Prevention, autism affects an estimated one in thirty-six children in the United States. Einstein is among the many famous scientists considered to have been on the autism spectrum, along with many artists, musicians, mathematicians, and designers.

Much later, when I was a graduate student in animal science at Arizona State University, I had another experience with cattle that helped me begin to understand why my mind worked differently than other people's minds.

The cattle handlers at a nearby ranch had a problem. They had set up a system to get their cows vaccinated—the cows would walk through a chute and at the end would receive their shots—but every time the handlers tried to send them through the chute, the cows would slow down or try to turn around. I was asked to help the handlers discover why this kept happening.

As I stood above the chute alongside the handlers, I watched the cows stop in their tracks. They did *not* want to walk forward. The cattle handlers had to yell, hit, and sometimes use electric prods to keep the cows moving through the chute.

What was going on? I jumped down into the chute to find out. The cattle handlers were surprised! But once inside, I immediately saw what was happening. There was a shiny metal chain dangling over the top of the chute. When the cows saw the sunlight bounce off the chain, they weren't sure what it was, so they stopped. I climbed back out of the chute and told the handlers what I had seen. As soon as they removed the chain, the cows started moving forward. No more yelling or prodding was necessary. To me, getting inside the chute was the obvious thing to do. I knew I had to *see* things from the cows' point of view to understand and solve the problem. None of the cattle handlers had thought to do that. Back then, I thought that everyone else thought visually the same way I did. It wasn't until I was in my thirties that I realized there are different kinds of thinkers, which explains why jumping in the chute was the most natural thing for me to do but not for everyone. It would have never occurred to me that you could study types of thinking or that there were all sorts of names for these different ways of thinking.

Verbal Thinkers

Do you think in words more than in pictures? Do you keep your assignments orderly and well organized? Do you always remember to hand in your homework? Are you good at keeping track of time? Do you keep your room neat, with everything in its place? Do you learn best by reading books and listening? Then you might be a verbal thinker.

Visual Thinkers

Do you think in pictures more than in words? Are you the one in your class who can take a random pile of art supplies and create something amazing? Does your backpack look messy, but you can still find anything you need inside it? Do you learn best from images, charts, and diagrams? Do you like puzzles, chess, and sports statistics? Then you might be a visual thinker.

Can You Be Both?

Most people use a combination of visual- and verbal-thinking skills. Fewer people are on the extreme ends of the spectrum. Photo-realistic visual thinkers like me are at one end, and totally verbal people like my book agent are at the other end. We'll talk about that more later in this chapter.

Finding the Visual Thinkers

When I realized that I was a visual thinker, I decided to conduct my own informal surveys to find out if other people also thought in pictures. By asking enough people the same questions, I hoped to identify fellow visual thinkers.

I started by asking people to describe their home using lots of visual details, like the colors of the walls and how many bedrooms it had. Almost everyone I asked was able to describe their home in detail. I knew that they couldn't *all* be visual thinkers. That seemed unlikely. Scientific experiments require trial and error, refining experiments over time and testing results. I suspected my question was too easy. To prove my hypothesis about different kinds of thinking, I needed to go back to the drawing board and change my tactic. Driving by the church in my town, I looked up and saw the steeple and it immediately struck me that I would use it for my next test question. Almost everyone knows what a steeple looks like, but it's not something you see every day. It's familiar, but not too familiar. When I asked people to describe a steeple, some were able to answer in almost photographic detail, describing the tower, the base, the spire, and the weathervane, as if they were standing right next to one. Others cited specific steeples, often naming several actual churches. In contrast, there were also people who had a harder time describing the physical characteristics of a steeple. In one extreme case, I asked a speech therapist I met at an autism conference to describe a steeple, and all she could picture were two lines connected to make a point like a witch's hat. She was excellent with language but wasn't able to visualize like the others.

A third group responded somewhere in between. They were able to describe a steeple but with fewer details. This group was a mix of verbal and visual thinkers.

You can try this yourself. Make a list from memory of as many descriptive words as you can about your room. What's in it, how large is it, what color are the walls—every detail. Make sure you are nowhere near your room when you compile your list.

Then, from memory as well, write down as many descriptive words as you can about a steeple—its height, color, location, and any more details you can think of.

Compare your answers. If you were able to describe the steeple with lots of details, you might be more of a visual thinker, because they are more challenging to recall than a space you're in every day. If you struggled with the steeple but had great recall on your room, you likely balance verbal and visual thinking. If you struggled recalling *both*, then you are more likely a verbal thinker. Words come first, pictures second.

Over the years, I've conducted other informal surveys. I show this picture and caption when I visit children in elementary schools and when I speak to adult teachers and school administrators.

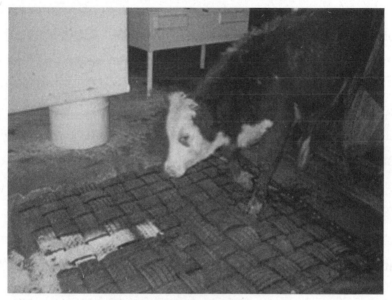

Do you see the cow looking at the sunbeam?

Then I ask both groups the same question: Do you see the cow looking at the sunbeam? When I ask kids, half the hands go up. When I ask adults, almost no hands go up. The adults focus on the *words* of the caption. The kids focus on the *picture*. From my informal study, it seems that many more kids are visual thinkers than adults. Some researchers believe that we all start as visual thinkers and as we grow up, language takes over. By four years old, most of us can speak in full sentences and have a vocabulary of over one thousand words. It seems that as language skills increase, visual skills decrease. The exceptions to this are visual thinkers, who, throughout their lives, primarily process information through pictures.

Scientists Laurent Mottron and Sylvie Belleville have also observed that, in addition to kids, another group of people are often strong visual thinkers: those with autism. They discovered that autistic adults pick up on small visual details in their environment faster than those without autism. And when another group of scientists led by Uta Frith and Amitta Shah compared how well autistic people and non-autistic people were able to arrange colorful blocks into patterns, those with autism were more successful. Both these teams of scientists confirmed that people with autism are often visual thinkers.

Dreaming Differently

My dreams also come to me in pictures. They resemble silent movies, only in color. They have lots of pictures and few words. Sometimes I dream that I'm on a steep roof or riding a bike. I also have a recurring dream of trying to get to the airport, but a huge visual roadblock— like a giant crater in the middle of the highway—makes me late.

The next time you remember a dream, write it down as soon as you wake up. Was the dream a series of images, was there a story, was it silent or did people talk? If you keep a notebook of your dreams, you might discover patterns about the way dreams come to you, in pictures or stories, silently or with words. It may provide yet another clue about what kind of thinker you are.

At the extreme ends of the spectrum are people with two unique conditions, aphantasia and hyperphantasia. A person with aphanta-sia has no or almost no ability to access visual imagery. When they see an idea expressed with pictures, charts, or diagrams, they have a harder time understanding it. At the other extreme, a person with hyperphantasia imagines an overabundance of visual images. When they are asked to describe a memory, they can do so with minutely detailed imagery. By studying people with these types of conditions, scientists have been able to learn more about how the brain works. I appreciate something neurologist Adam Zeman said: "This is not a disorder, as far as I can see. It's an intriguing variation in human experience." To Zeman, thinking or dreaming one way or another is not an illness or a problem—it's just different.

It's a Verbal Thinker's World

My first language is pictures. My second language is words. The problem for me is that we live in a culture that emphasizes ver-bal communication. Teachers lecture. Politicians use speeches to get their message across. Religious leaders use sermons. And the people who give us the news are called talking heads. Visual thinkers like me are forced to adapt.

It's like I am a tourist in a foreign country who knows a bit of the language, but it's not my mother tongue. With a lot of coach-ing, tutoring, and hard work, I've learned to speak and communicate throughout my life in school, college, graduate school, and eventually in the workplace. But this didn't come naturally. As a child I learned how to modulate my voice by imitating other people. I learned to say "Hello!" in a bright, inviting way instead of my flat or monotone voice, which is something many people with autism struggle with. We may be very enthusiastic about something, but it sounds like we aren't particularly interested because of our speech. We also struggle with picking up on verbal cues. As a result, our social skills are compromised, and we interview poorly for jobs even though we may be more qualified than a verbal thinker. As an adult, I still wrestle with this. Sometimes jokes go over my head, especially if the punchline is based on wordplay. You might have heard the classic joke:

—What's white and black and red all over?

—A newspaper.

It's hard for me to comprehend because my mind is busy picturing shades of red and a physical newspaper. It takes a while for me to catch up and realize that wordplay is involved—"Oh, the word 'red' sounds like the word 'read.' I get it!" I also get lost when people speak too quickly for me to catch the nuances, either subtle gestures or changes in expression. Irony is often lost on me.

This "language barrier" can unintentionally give kids who are visual thinkers unique challenges in school. Imagine a classroom where a teacher is talking fast to get through a lesson. The more verbal students can probably keep up, but the visual-thinking student is still trying to translate the lesson into their own "language" of imagery and soon falls behind. Additionally, tests are also mostly language based, written in words, without any pictures to convey the questions. A visual-thinking student has to translate the word-based questions into their own visual way of thinking, and only then can they answer them. It's like having only right-handed desks in school, with no lefty desks for people who write left-handed. They are already at a disadvantage.

Denver-based psychologist Linda Kreger Silverman has spent decades studying different learning styles. When she speaks to educators about different types of learning styles, she will often show her audiences two images:

She calls one the "filer" and the other the "piler." The filer keeps everything in its place, neat and orderly. The piler keeps everything in what appears to be a mess, without an obvious system of organization.

Filers keep everything in its place, neat and orderly.

Pilers keep everything in what appears to be a mess, without an obvious system of organization.

Silverman explains that the filer is not necessarily smarter than the piler, and the piler is not necessarily smarter than the filer. They simply have different skill sets.

If you made the person with the messy pile organize their papers, they would never find anything again. My office is like that, with towering piles that, to verbal thinkers, look like a disaster area. But I can easily locate any paper. To me, it's organized. My agent once visited me in my home and wanted to straighten out my piles. She said she could never work with all that clutter. I told her not to touch a thing. That would have been ruinous for me. I know where every paper is in my "piles." I can visualize them.

For some reason, our culture gives more credit to the filers. Many assume that the filer kid is the smarter or more capable kid. Teachers often give out extra-credit points to students who have the neatest-looking notes, handwriting, or cubbies, and parents struggle to teach their kids to clean up their rooms and make them look orderly. Many parents and teachers confuse tidiness with intelligence. Why is one way of organizing thoughts considered better than the other?

The Messy Scientist

Albert Einstein didn't learn to speak until he was three years old, and one of his elementary school teachers described him as "mentally slow and unsociable."

Yet he grew up to discover many revolutionary scientific theories, including the theory of relativity, and in 1922 he won the Nobel Prize for his ideas on the photoelectric effect. Considered one of the most brilliant scientists of all time, he was also famous for his untidy appearance and wild hair. There is some debate whether Einstein actually said, "If a cluttered desk is a sign of a cluttered mind, of what, then, is an empty desk a sign?" Whether he did or didn't, I think he must have been a piler, like me.

More recently, the term "neurotypical" is being used to describe people who develop along more predictable lines, and "neurodivergent" is used for people who have different strengths and challenges. In my lifetime, various words such as "crippled," "handicapped," and "disabled" were used to describe people who do not conform to what we call "normal." "Normal" is a strange word. What *is* normal? Someone with curly hair or someone with straight hair? Someone who is good at sports or someone who is good at art? "Normal" is a term that I shy away from because defining what is normal is as unhelpful as asking what the "normal" size of a dog is. A Chihuahua or a Great Dane? I like the terms "neurotypical" and "neurodivergent" because they acknowledge the many ways our different brains work.

On the TV sitcom *The Big Bang Theory*, the character Sheldon Cooper was clearly brilliant but lacking in social skills. He spoke in a monotone (like I did when I was younger) and didn't understand basic human emotions. But among his scientist friends, he was probably the one whose off-the-charts intelligence could save the planet. Sheldon's nerdy qualities were seen as funny on TV, but in real life, kids who think and act like Sheldon are often bullied—no laughing matter. As a child, I was socially awkward myself and was badly bullied in middle school. I didn't find a true group of friends until I found fellow "Sheldons."

I once worked with a guy who was extremely socially awkward and had no college degree. He started as a car mechanic but then went on to develop about twenty patents, own a metal shop, and invent custom-designed manufacturing equipment. I worked with another man who was dyslexic and stuttered a lot. He did very poorly in high school, but a single welding class set him on his path.

He went on to design and sell high-end, patented equipment all over the world. I wonder how these neurodivergent people would get along in school if they were students today.

The Know-It-All

As a child, Elon Musk ran out of books to read in the library. His mother said he memorized every book he read. His advanced intelligence drew the ire of bullies, who would follow him home and throw soda cans at his head. One time a group of bullies pushed him down the stairs and beat him up. But Musk's abilities could also be considered superpowers: extreme concentration, photographic memory, single-minded focus, and a likely combination of extreme object and spatial visual thinking. He taught himself to code and at twelve years old, he sold his first video game for $500.

Musk famously dropped out of graduate school and went to Silicon Valley, where he founded more than one computer company, including PayPal. He built Tesla into a trillion-dollar electric car company and spurred on other car companies to develop electric cars, which are better for the planet. He has also made it a life goal to develop a multi-planetary civilization. To that end, he created SpaceX. In 2022, he successfully launched 180 rockets into orbit. His current mission is to colonize Mars. You get the feeling that if anyone can do this, it's Musk.

More recently, Elon Musk also acquired Twitter. I admire his achievements with rockets and electric cars, but his management of the social media platform has created controversies. He entered an arena of social and emotional factors that can be more complex than rocket science. Maybe he should have remained in the world of rockets and cars.

Journey to the Center of the Brain

Some people mistakenly believe that visual thinking is the same as seeing. Visual and verbal thinking happen in the brain. The brain processes what we see and how we communicate. Over the past centuries, there have been many scientists who have studied the brain and made major discoveries. Because our brains are located inside our heads, this can be challenging to do. It's not like scientists can just open your skull and look inside. Instead, scientists have discovered different solutions for studying the brain.

Animal studies. There have been many animal studies, sometimes unethical ones, that have led to brain discoveries. For example, when David Ferrier removed the prefrontal lobes of monkeys' brains, he found that while the monkeys were still able to walk and jump, their personalities were profoundly changed. He also became the first scientist to be tried under the Cruelty to Animals Act of 1876.

Observational studies. Over the decades, patients with brain injuries have given scientists opportunities to learn about brain function. By observing where in the brain the physical injuries occurred, and then seeing which of the patients' abilities were impacted, scientists could conclude which parts of the brain controlled which abilities.

The Case of Phineas Gage

On September 13, 1848, railway worker Phineas Gage became the most famous patient in neuroscience. That day, his crew was cutting a tunnel for a new railway. Gage used an iron rod to pack some explosives used to blast rock and make way for the railroad tracks. They exploded accidentally, sending the rod through Gage's cheekbone and out the top of his skull. He miraculously survived, and despite his severe brain injury, he was still able to see, walk, and talk. But he also had major personality changes.

Phineas Gage's prefrontal cortex was damaged after an iron rod went through his head.

He started cursing regularly. He acted unkindly toward others. And his friends at the time said that Gage was "no longer Gage."

His case was critical in providing a link between brain trauma and personality change, and it gave scientists their first glimpse into the function of the prefrontal cortex.

Today, more than 170 years later, researchers at UCLA's Laboratory of Neuro Imaging are still using Gage's case to find out more about the effects of brain injuries, and his skull is on exhibit at Harvard Medical School's campus.

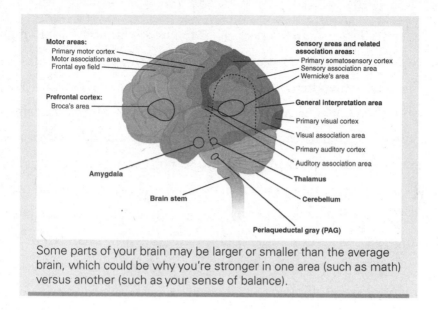

Motor areas:
Primary motor cortex
Motor association area
Frontal eye field

Prefrontal cortex:
Broca's area

Amygdala

Brain stem

Sensory areas and related association areas:
Primary somatosensory cortex
Sensory association area
Wernicke's area

General interpretation area

Primary visual cortex

Visual association area

Primary auditory cortex

Auditory association area

Thalamus

Cerebellum

Periaqueductal gray (PAG)

Some parts of your brain may be larger or smaller than the average brain, which could be why you're stronger in one area (such as math) versus another (such as your sense of balance).

New tools. Over time, tools have been invented that allow scientists to peer inside the brain. Advanced techniques like PET scans, EEGs, CT scans, MRIs, and fMRIs produce images of the brain and have been used to diagnose brain injuries, tumors, dementia, strokes, and more.

I have had my own brain scanned many times. As a scientist, I have a tremendous urge to explore my brain, to see if I can unlock some of the mysteries of my autism and better understand how I think. I had my first MRI (which stands for magnetic resonance imaging) brain scan in 1987, done by Eric Courchesne at the University of California, San Diego. The MRI took beautiful, detailed pictures of my brain. When I saw them, I exclaimed, "Journey to the center of my brain!" From this scan, I learned why I had balance problems. My cerebellum (the part of the brain that controls balance) was 20 percent smaller than the average brain. Another MRI scan of my brain showed that my amygdala (the brain's emotion center) was three times larger than average. That might explain why I had high levels of anxiety before I started treating it with antidepressants.

The scans that blew my mind were done at the University of Pittsburgh by Walter Schneider, the inventor of diffusion tensor imaging (DTI). That scan created the clearest images I had ever seen of my brain, and I learned a lot from it. For example, Dr. Schneider and I noticed that my speech circuits were much smaller than most people's. This might explain why my speech was delayed as a child. In contrast, the section of my brain that controls visualization was huge—400 percent larger than most people's, and proof positive that I am a visual thinker.

Brainiacs

1776: Francesco Gennari froze human brains and dissected them. He discovered that the brain had different parts that did different things.

1861: Paul Broca discovered the speech center in the brain. A person with an injury to the Broca region will often be fully able to understand language but unable to speak.

1874: Carl Wernicke discovered the area of the brain where language comprehension happens. A person with an injury to the Wernicke area will often have scrambled thoughts but still be able to speak.

1881: David Ferrier conducted experiments on animal brains and discovered the part of the brain that controls movement.

1904–1905: Tatsuji Inouye worked with soldiers who had been shot in the brain during battle. By recording exactly what part of the patient's brain the bullet had damaged, and seeing how the patient's vision was impacted, he was able to figure out which part of the brain controls sight. Today we call it the occipital lobe.

1904–1905: British neurologists developed a diagram of the brain using new information they learned from working with wounded soldiers.

1971: Godfrey Hounsfield invented the CT scan. It uses radiation to take detailed X-rays of brain structures.

1977: Raymond Damadian invented the first MRI scanner. It takes detailed pictures of brain structures using strong magnetic fields and radio waves, and it does not expose the patient to radiation.

1990: Seiji Ogawa discovered the technique that led to the development of the fMRI (functional magnetic resonance imaging). Building on existing MRI technology, fMRI can scan brains and measure which parts a person uses when they complete tasks.

Seeing Is Believing, but It's Not Visual Thinking

About a third of our brain is taken up by the occipital lobe, which contains part of the visual cortex. These are the parts of the brain that are responsible for seeing and visualizing. Often people make the mistake of thinking that "seeing" and "visualizing'" are interchangeable.

Seeing is when your eyes take in the information you are literally looking at. You see a tree and your brain translates that information as a tree. Visualizing is when you *imagine something that isn't in front of you.* You do it all the time. Think of a tree right now: for most people, a vague image of a tree comes to mind or maybe a tree you saw earlier in the day. For extreme visual thinkers like me, we tend to see a series of photorealistic images of trees.

Bats have provided one of the best analogies to describe how visual thinking works. You may have heard the phrase "blind as a bat," but bats are not blind. However, what makes them so successful at hunting for food and flying at night is their enhanced hearing abilities. Bats make clicking noises and use the echoes of those sounds to detect what's going on in front of them. They "see" with sound. We call this echolocation. About 25 percent of blind people echolocate as well, by making clicking sounds with their mouths, snapping their fingers, or tapping with a cane. They aren't seeing in the way we usually think about sight; they are visualizing patterns of sound.

Right Brain, Left Brain

In 2019, neuroscientist and cognitive psychologist Qunlin Chen scanned the brains of 502 people as they completed tasks like making a toy elephant more fun to play with, drawing ten figures, and coming up with alternative uses for a can. He discovered that people who used visual thinking to complete their tasks mostly showed activity in the right side of their brains, while those who used verbal thinking tended to use the left side, meaning one hemisphere in the brain is more dominant than the other.

People who identify as "right brain" consider themselves to be more creative and emotional, while "left brain" thinkers identify as more logical and analytical. But it isn't as simple as that. Take the case of Matthew Whitaker, a gifted musician who was born blind. When he was three, his grandfather gave him a small electronic keyboard, and he immediately started playing songs on it like "Twinkle, Twinkle Little Star." At the age of five, Matthew became the youngest student to be admitted to the Filomen M. D'Agostino Greenberg Music School, which specializes in teaching blind and visually impaired students. Based on what we know from Chen's study, one might think the part of Matthew's brain that is typically used for sight would be unusable. But when Matthew's brain was scanned while he played keyboard, Charles Limb, who runs the UCSF Sound and Music Perception Lab, discovered something amazing. The part of Mathew's brain that is normally reserved for sight in other people was instead being utilized to perceive music.

It would be nice if the world divided into right-brain and left-brain thinkers. But the brain is much more complex than that, and communication between the two hemispheres of the brain isn't a simple equation. For example, Chen has found that a balance between the sides of the brain can make a person's verbal thinking stronger. All different combinations are possible: you might be a verbal thinker who is also good at math, or a rocket scientist who likes to write poetry.

The Different Kinds of Visualizers

Scientists have discovered that among visual thinkers, there are at least two subsets. Object visual thinkers, like me, who think in pictures. And spatial visual thinkers, who think in patterns and often are mathematically inclined. It's important not to clump them together.

I saw this in action first-hand in the food-processing industry, where I've worked for my entire career. The spatial visual thinkers have advanced degrees. They are the ones who design parts of the food-processing plants that require advanced mathematics, such as boilers, refrigeration units for chilling the meat, and water systems. In contrast, the object visual thinkers almost never have advanced degrees. They are the ones who build and invent specialized mechanical equipment such as packaging machines. It's the collaboration between these two types of thinkers that makes things work, gets things built, and allows the plant to operate smoothly.

Object Visual Thinkers

Do you have friends who like to build massive structures with Legos or take things apart and put them back together? Do you know anyone more fascinated by the pulleys used to draw the curtains on a stage or the set design than the play itself? That was me. I never would have dreamed of reciting lines or acting, but I could show off my skills designing and constructing sets. Often, we say these kinds of people are "good with their hands." The reason they are good with their hands is because they tend to be object thinkers. They easily visualize the way things work. Object visualizers often excel in careers such as graphic design, art, mechanical engineering, and architecture.

Spatial Visual Thinkers

Do you know anyone who can do difficult math problems in their head or can recite every baseball player's statistics without hesitating? Do you know anyone who could code or play Mozart sonatas on their violin at age six or by ear? It's likely they are spatial thinkers capable of seeing patterns whole, where others need step-by-step instruction. If you think about why you are good at some things and not others, it's usually because of the way your brain processes information. Spatial thinkers excel in careers such as coding, mathematics, accounting, chemistry, physics, music, and inventing.

Researcher Maria Kozhevnikov demonstrated this distinction through a series of groundbreaking tests. In one, she showed a group of visual thinkers the image below and asked them to describe what they saw.

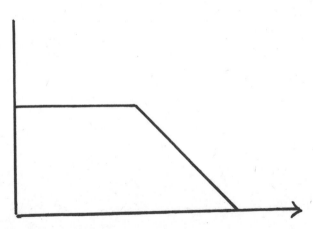

When you look at this image, describe what you see. Here is a graph of an object's motion. Imagine a real situation depicted in the graph. Since I am an object visualizer, I visualized coasting down a snowy hill on my sled. A spatial visualizer may see a more abstract depiction of motion.

When the object visualizers looked at the drawing, they imagined a real-life situation, such as a ball rolling down a ramp. They pictured a real ball in motion. When the spatial visualizers looked at the picture, they imagined the movement of the ball, not the ball itself. They think in abstractions, which are the *ideas* of things. As soon as I read about Kozhevnikov's work, I knew immediately that I was an object thinker. And when I look at the image on the previous page, I connect it with a physical activity in the real world: riding my sled down a hill.

Early in my career, I impressed my colleagues by figuring out how to draft complex buildings in just a couple days. I had never taken a drafting class. To learn to read blueprints, I took a set of drawings for an existing factory and walked through the place while looking at the drawings. I had to figure out how to relate the real things I saw, like columns that support the building's roof, to shapes on the floor plan. I knew that the best way for me to do that would be to traipse through the place and see the columns and structures for myself. This was pure object thinking. If I can see the actual thing, I can draw it or build it.

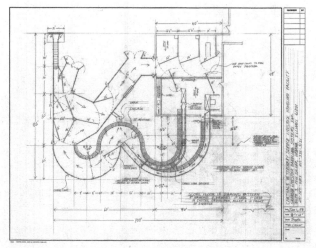

A blueprint I created without taking a drafting class.

In contrast, spatial thinkers can automatically morph two-dimensional renderings (like a blueprint) into three-dimensional structures—sort of like Tony Stark does in the Iron Man movies when he touches the screen in his garage workshop and a 3D image pops up.

In another groundbreaking test by Kozhevnikov and Olesya Blazhenkova, middle schoolers and high school students gifted in the arts and sciences were given a single prompt: draw an unknown planet. That's all the information they were given.

The art students (object thinkers) created vivid, fantastical drawings. Their drawings included highly creative pictures that spanned the globe, from Egyptian pyramids to Antarctic penguins. One showed a unique crystal planet, and in a third drawing the students created a fantastic building. Meanwhile, the scientists (spatial thinkers) focused more on the practical functions of their planet, like gravity, chemistry, and biodiversity. They used fewer colors, and their drawings were more realistic than fantastical. One thing the object and spatial visualizers had in common was that they carefully planned out their drawings. The verbal thinkers, on the other hand, did not plan. Their drawings lacked imagery and resembled splotchy abstract paintings. Instead of visual detail, they wrote the descriptions of their planets, then changed their minds and erased them, thinking that using words was against the rules. Verbal thinkers tend to be rule followers. This makes sense, because rules are usually word based and follow a clear logic of action and consequences. In many ways, being a rule follower helps you in school and in the workplace, and it's important to follow rules to be a good citizen. But great art and innovation often requires breaking the rules. Pablo Picasso, known for his brilliant abstract paintings, said, "Learn the rules like a pro, so you can break them like an artist."

The Marine Corps has some of the best truck mechanics and engineers in the world. They can fix and design anything. But the leaders of the Marines wanted to know: Could their mechanics and engineers work under extreme circumstances? Would they be able to improvise in stressful conditions?

They reached out to Brad Halsey, the owner of Building Momentum, a company that focuses on leadership and problem-solving training. They wanted him to create a program that would help them weed out the mechanics and engineers who couldn't meet those demanding challenges. Halsey was an ideal pick for the job. He had spent almost a year as a soldier in the Iraq War, where he had often made tools out of things he found in local junkyards. He once took a bunch of balloons, added fake sensors to them, and launched them into the air to confuse the opposition, who was trying to shoot down U.S. Army surveillance balloons.

Halsey created the program for the Marine Corps and named it Innovation Boot Camp. Those who participated in it had another name for it: Hell Week. During the program, Halsey gathered the engineers and mechanics and presented them with many challenges. One day he gave them a pile of junk. It had things like pipes, tires, and old machine parts in it. Then he told them they had to make a simple, working car from it and said, "GO!"

Both the mechanics and the engineers got to work, hammering, assembling, and designing. The pressure was on. And when the time was up and the mechanics and engineers showed off their improvised cars, Halsey made a remarkable discovery. The truck mechanics' results were much better than those of the engineers. Even though the engineers had impressive degrees from prestigious universities like Stanford and MIT, the mechanics had made better cars. He later explained that "engineers tend to overthink" and could not innovate as quickly.

My interpretation is that the truck mechanics were likely object thinkers who had no problem working with their hands and thinking on their feet. They could *see* the pile of junk and figure out how to make it into something else with ease. In contrast, the engineers were spatial thinkers. They were excellent at designing something back in the lab using drawings and computer renderings, testing ideas through multiple simulations.

So, if you are going to be in the middle of a war and need someone to come up with quick solutions, it's more likely that an object visual thinker is the one to come to your rescue.

The Visual Thinker's Strengths and Challenges

When you compare visual thinking to verbal thinking, you quickly discover that each one has its strengths and its challenges. For instance, I think more slowly than many verbal thinkers. I don't do well on timed tests because my brian needs time to create pictures and process information. On the other hand, I notice and remember an exceptional number of details. When I was in elementary school, I loved embroidery class, and even though that was years ago, I can still recall details of the silk thread that I used. It was different colors and made from three strands. When I tell people this, many will ask me, "How can you remember that?!" They are amazed that I have complete recall of such small details. But I do. Because I can "see" the threads in my imagination, I can tell you how many there are.

I can feel and see the needle piercing the fabric. My visual thinking gives me remarkable recall.

Another strength of my visual thinking is a heightened level of problem-solving. My mind uses what I call "bottom-up" rather than "top-down" thinking. My mind is like a visual database. It groups many images into categories to create an understanding of a concept. When I was little, I used size to differentiate dogs from cats: the larger animals went into one section of the spreadsheet under the category of "dog," and smaller animals went into the category of "cat." When my neighbors got a tiny dachshund, that upended my system, so I reorganized and started differentiating cats from dogs by using another category: barking versus meowing. This approach is called bottom-up thinking because it is built on compiling facts to reach a conclusion.

As an adult, I still use bottom-up thinking. When I speak to audiences about autism, often a parent will approach me for advice about how to help their autistic child learn to speak. Before I answer, I'll ask lots of questions, like: How old is your child? Can they use a fork and knife? Can they take turns playing a game? What do the parents do for a living? It can be a little like the Twenty Questions game. Every new answer gives me another fact that I build and build on until I can get a full picture of the silent child. Once I understand all those facts, I can then suggest some things that might help. If I asked *no* questions, I would have no idea how to help them. If the child is seventeen years old, it would be useless for me to talk to the parents about early educational programs for little three-year-olds. Being a bottom-up thinker keeps me grounded in the facts.

Top-down thinking, on the other hand, can sometimes cause people to overgeneralize and in turn be inaccurate. Top-down thinkers tend to group too many distinct categories together. If they were organizing animals, they'd put cats, dogs, chimpanzees, and whales all into one large category of "animals" and not be able to accurately describe their differences because they haven't dug in to look at the details.

Owen Suskind lost his ability to speak at three years old and was diagnosed with autism. His remarkable story is told in the 2016 documentary film *Life, Animated*. Owen loved Disney movies like *Aladdin* and *Beauty and the Beast* and watched them over and over. When he slowly started to regain speech, he only repeated lines from the movies. It wasn't clear if Owen was copying what he heard or if the words had meaning. He was correctly diagnosed as autistic, but his doctors didn't know how to reach him. They didn't know enough about him. One day, on a hunch, Owen's father picked up a puppet of his son's favorite Disney character, Iago, the parrot from *Aladdin*. Using the puppet's voice, the father started a conversation with his son. Owen was able to express his feelings and ideas using what he learned about life from the movies, not just "parroting" what he had heard. From there, Owen started communicating using all the Disney characters to express a wide range of interests and thoughts. No doctor could have prescribed "Use an Iago puppet!" But someone like his father, who knew the specific facts about Owen's interests and obsessions, was able to use bottom-up thinking and make the connection. Today, researchers at Yale University in conjunction with Jim Henson's Muppets are researching the use of puppets to help reach children with autism.

Visual Thinking Saves the Day

Visual thinking has often helped scientists discover new ideas and solve complex mysteries.

When chemist August Kekulé went to sleep one time, he dreamed of a snake forming a ring by holding its tail in its mouth. When he woke up, he thought about that image more, and it led him to innovate the idea of the benzene ring. In organic chemistry, the benzene ring is an important concept that explains the structure of compounds such as gasoline. Because of Kekulé's visual thinking, we know that it has the same circular shape as a snake holding its tail.

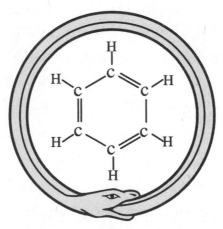

Kekulé's dream of a snake inspired the benzene ring.

Geneticist Kim Nasmyth made a major scientific discovery when he was threading his ropes into loops in preparation for a climb. In his mind's eye, he was able to make the connection when he visualized the ropes as the long strands of DNA looped inside a cell. This led him to propose innovative new theories that help us understand DNA today.

When astronauts went for a spacewalk to check on the Hubble telescope, they were horrified to find that the telescope's surface had numerous dents, made by tiny pieces of space trash crashing into it. Hubble's engineers had always known that space trash might damage the telescope, but until the astronauts shared the video of the dents with them, they had never *seen* the dents and didn't quite understand the issue. As one engineer said, "I don't think we thought about what it *looked* like." Another engineer was so astonished by the images of the dents that he played the video over and over, trying to learn as much as he could from looking at them. Visualizing the problem led the engineers to develop solutions to address it. One small step for mankind, one giant leap because of visual thinking.

What Kind of Thinker Are You?

People often ask me: Is there a way to know if someone is a verbal or visual thinker?

Signs of a person's thinking style often show up when they are about six to eight years old. If they have a tendency for visual thinking at that age, they might create beautiful drawings that are highly detailed and realistic, enjoy building with toys like blocks, Legos, and erector sets, or putting things together with materials they find around the house, such as cardboard or wood. As a child, Stephen Hawking took apart model trains and airplanes before making a simple computer out of recycled clock and telephone parts. He grew up to be a world-famous physicist. Pioneering computer scientist and mathematician Grace Murray Hopper took apart all seven of the clocks in her family home when she was a kid. Both future scientists were showing early signs of visual thinking.

There is no X-ray or medical test that can tell you if you are a verbal or visual thinker, or a combination of both. But this quiz by Linda Kreger Silverman and her team can help you figure it out for yourself. Answer each of the following yes or no questions and tally them up when you are done. If you are not sure, just make your best guess, but try to answer them all.

	YES	NO
1. Do you think mainly in pictures instead of words?	___	___
2. Do you know things without being able to explain how or why?	___	___
3. Do you solve problems in unusual ways?	___	___
4. Do you have a vivid imagination?	___	___
5. Do you remember what you see and forget what you hear?	___	___
6. Are you terrible at spelling?	___	___
7. Can you visualize objects from different perspectives?	___	___
8. Do you have trouble organizing?	___	___
9. Do you often lose track of time?	___	___
10. Would you rather read a map than follow verbal directions?	___	___
11. Do you remember how to get to places you've visited only once?	___	___
12. Is your handwriting slow and difficult for others to read?	___	___
13. Can you feel what others are feeling?	___	___

14. Are you musically, artistically, or mechanically inclined?   ___ ___

15. Do you know more than others think you know?   ___ ___

16. Do you hate speaking in front of a group?   ___ ___

17. Did you feel smarter as you got older?   ___ ___

18. Are you addicted to your computer?   ___ ___

If you answered "yes" to ten or more of the above questions, you are very likely to be a visual thinker.

Remember, very few people will reply "yes" to all the questions. I replied "yes" to sixteen out of eighteen, which puts me at the far end of the visual-thinking spectrum. My assistant is a highly verbal person, and she answered "yes" to only four of the questions. Most people will likely fall somewhere in the middle; these people balance both kinds of thinking.

After you take the test, you might have a clearer sense as to why you are good at some things and not others, why you gravitate to words or pictures. Sometimes students will say, "I'm bad at math" or "I hate reading." It's very possible that there is a reason why some things come more easily to some people and not others. Knowing how you think is an important clue to the way your brain works and might even suggest a successful career path.

But as you'll see in the next chapter, that's unfortunately *not* what schools in the United States are doing. They are often doing the opposite. By trying to teach everyone the same way and using standardized tests that favor verbal thinkers, we are screening out our visual thinkers.

CHAPTER TWO
Screened Out

WHEN I WAS IN FIFTH GRADE, MY FAVORITE CLASS WAS shop. (Basically, where you learn to build things and use tools.) Back when I went to school in the 1960s, shop was typically for boys, and home economics (where you learn "domestic" arts such as cooking and sewing) was for girls. I was lucky that our shop teacher, Mr. Patriarca, was open-minded enough to let me join his class along with one other girl.

I can vividly remember the shop room and its hammers, screwdrivers, and drills hanging in a neat row. In shop, I discovered how much I loved working with my hands. I learned to make a wooden boat and a small table in the shape of a violin, all from just pieces of wood, screws, a handsaw, glue, and my own efforts. Most importantly, no matter what project we were working on, I learned how to use tools and how to make things.

I also learned to respect my materials. The shop room was always neat and orderly, and Mr. Patriarca insisted that we do our part to keep it that way. "Leave this place cleaner than you found it!" he would repeat over and over. So, at the end of every class, I would put my tools back in their neat rows. This was a real contrast from my room at home. My mother was always asking me to clean it, but I never seemed to get around to it. But in Mr. Patriarca's class, I made sure to put away every tool and sweep up every scrap.

Another favorite class of mine was home economics, where I learned to sew. I loved it almost as much as I loved shop for the same reason: we got to work with our hands. I would take an activity over textbooks any day. I was an active kid and doing physical things was both enjoyable and allowed me to focus. In third grade, I learned how to use a needle and thread, and in fourth grade, I had a toy sewing machine that made rudimentary stitches. By seventh grade, I was using full-sized sewing machines, which really fired up my technical mind.

The Machine That Sewed

One of my favorite inventors is Elias Howe, who created the lockstitch sewing machine. At 250 stitches a minute, Howe's machine was able to stich in one hour what otherwise took expert seamstresses 14.5 hours to sew.

Elias Howe, inventor of the lock-stitch sewing machine.

At just sixteen years old, Howe worked in a machinist's shop. Later, he started work at a textile mill, where he learned about fabrics and stitching. These hands-on experiences gave him the knowledge he needed to invent a machine that transformed the garment industry. Alongside other revolutionary inventions like the cotton gin, Howe's lockstitch sewing machine ushered in the age of cheaper, faster clothing production.

If Howe had been a student in today's classroom, I'm not sure he ever would have come up with his invention, because he'd never be given those same types of hands-on opportunities.

Howe's revolutionary invention.

When I was a student, both shop and home economics were available to students at nearly every public school in the United States. But if you went to public school in the 1990s or after, there's a good chance you never had the opportunity to learn hands-on skills in school. Especially after 2001, when the reform bill known as No Child Left Behind was made into law, finding these classes was next to impossible.

The new bill mainly focused on tests. The original goal was to raise national academic standards through testing. But in practice, it led to what some people referred to as "drill, kill, bubble fill." Teachers were encouraged to teach students only what they needed to know to fill in those little bubbles on the test sheets—and nothing more. Activities such as outdoor projects and field trips were cut. When I was growing up, field trips were a big deal. I vividly recall my elementary school trip to a car factory, where I got to watch an air wrench screw in all five bolts on a wheel at once. I couldn't believe that a machine could do so quickly what took my dad lots of sweat and time. I could have stared at that air wrench for hours. The budding clever engineer in me was inspired and on fire.

Just a Sidewalk Away

A very creative and motivated kindergarten teacher in New York City took her class on "field trips to the sidewalk," where she taught them everything from math to vocabulary to science and history. Whether you're in a rural community or a big city, your environment is filled with things you can learn about, from trees and fields to buses and skyscrapers. Today, field trips are being cut from the curriculum due to budget cuts. You don't need dollars to have a field trip—just curiosity and teachers who want to give their students exposure to new things. It's something you might be able to ask your teachers to try.

Finding Your Strengths

As I said in the introduction to this book, "What do you want to be when you grow up?" is probably the number one question adults ask kids. But the question I like best is: What are you good at? It's okay if you don't know yet. Exposure to lots of different kinds of things will help you find out. That's how it worked for me. My most impactful experience as a child happened when I was fifteen and had the chance to work on my aunt's ranch in Arizona.

I loved everything about it. The horses and cattle, the barn, and the big open sky all fascinated me, and my interest in them helped launch me on my career path. By working directly with animals and tools, I discovered my strengths. Without those experiences, I don't know how I would have found my talents.

I discovered a beautiful print shop in Maine called PrintCraft that specialized in nineteenth- and twentieth-century printmaking and antique letter presses. The owner, Lisa Pixley, proudly showed me how they worked. Each press had its own mechanical setup, and she expertly worked the foot pedals and hand pulls as she guided the paper through the drum of each machine. This took a great deal of mechanical expertise and an ability to work with her hands. I asked Lisa how she did in school, having a hunch that she was a visual thinker. She didn't do well, especially in math, specifically algebra, and had been put in special education classes. It had derailed her academic career for years. Fortunately, she discovered her love of printmaking on her own and became a master printer. Her visual skills were not recognized in school, but they fueled her creativity. I asked if she would take a visual-spatial test and she agreed. She scored as high as I did on it: pure visual thinker as I suspected. Pixley is a perfect example of an object thinker who wasn't recognized for her talents in school but who fortunately found her calling.

When schools cancel real-life experiences, students lose the opportunity to learn about careers they might never have heard of. Without exposure, how can anyone discover if they'd like to be a construction worker, an engineer, or a chef? The disappearance of these experiences has limited an entire generation of visual thinkers. There is no way for visual-thinking kids to find out what they're good at by sitting behind a desk all day. Plus, it's torture for kids like me who have excess energy and need to be doing and making things. These abilities need to be developed when kids are young. Here are some examples of people who were exposed at a young age to something that sparked a brilliant career.

It's not a coincidence that the Renaissance sculptor Michelangelo became the world's most celebrated sculptor. He was six when his mother died and he went to live with his nurse, where he benefited from exposure to her husband, a stonecutter. "Along with the milk of my nurse," he said, according to one of his biographers, "I received the knack of handling chisel and hammer, with which I make my figures." He sculpted *David*, a seventeen-foot-high youth in perfect proportion, carved in marble and considered to be one of the greatest works of art in the Western world.

Software inventor Bill Gates created his first computer programs at Seattle's Lakeside High School. Lakeside had a terminal and a few computers, which were just coming on the scene. More important, the administration allowed interested students to work on them. "Instead of teaching us about computers in the conventional sense, Lakeside just unleashed us," Gates said. Along with schoolmate Paul Allen, Gates started the computing behemoth Microsoft. "If there had been no Lakeside, there would have been no Microsoft."

Co-founder of Apple Computer and design/marketing genius Steve Jobs loved to tinker in his neighbor's garage (his neighbor worked at the electronics company Hewlett-Packard, and the garage was filled with all kinds of equipment). His own father had a base-ment workshop and instilled the idea that the inside of things needed to be as beautiful as the outside. I think Jobs must have been deeply influenced by his father's aesthetic combined with exposure to all that equipment. He and Steve Wozniak invented the Apple computer and iPhone. The beautiful packaging is a big part of the success of Apple products down to the fonts (typeface), which Jobs had studied before he dropped out of college.

Thomas Edison is one of my heroes. He was at the bottom of his class when his mother pulled him out of grade school and essentially homeschooled him. She supplied his lively mind with science books. To make money, the young Edison cobbled together local news articles and sold them as newspapers on the railroad, but he had also created a basement laboratory with more than two hundred chemicals. By twelve, the entrepreneur and scientist were fully merged. He held the record for the most patents, including the light bulb, phonograph, and motion-picture camera, and is one of our greatest inventors.

Another reason that removing hands-on learning was the worst choice schools could have made is that cutting them took away opportunities to learn real-life skills. For example, when I was in sewing class, I loved measuring fabric, cutting it accurately, and sewing it together. When I grew up and had a job putting together complicated livestock-handling systems, those skills helped me immensely. The same was true for my drawing skills. Learning to draw back in art class helps me draft detailed blueprints today.

Many of my college-level students have never had those same real-world opportunities. I recently had a student in my class who had never used a ruler to measure things. And in my professional work, I've started to see many strange problems pop up on drawings made by drafting technicians who have never learned to draw by hand. They don't always place the center of a circle in the center, for example. Or they leave out critical details on their blueprints, like reinforcing rods for strengthening concrete.

This is happening in other fields, too. A doctor I spoke with who trains up-and-coming surgeons told me that many of his students find it challenging to learn how to sew up simple cuts because they have never used a needle and thread. They never got to take sewing, like I did. We are losing skills in schools and at home. When I grew up, more people sewed their own clothes and mended them. Today, most of us buy clothes and get new ones when they need repair. That's fine; the problem is that we are losing a skill set we may need.

By taking away these classes, we are not just hurting these individuals; there is also a huge cost to our society. Sewing may not sound like a big deal, but our world is going to be in trouble if we don't address the lack of *all* kinds of skills and the people who can perform them, from construction workers to surgeons. We need this and future generations of workers to be able to build and repair infrastructure, overhaul energy and agriculture, create tools to combat climate change and pandemics, and develop robotics and AI. We need people with the imagination to invent our next-generation solutions.

Screen Time

There is no doubt in my mind that if I had been born thirty years later than I was, I would have become a video game addict. Autistic individuals are more prone to excessive video game playing, and I'm sure I would have found everything from *Mario Bros.* to *Minecraft* intoxicating.

Many parents confide in me that they can't get their kids away from screens. (That might be because the parents themselves are also glued to their screens!) Both adults and kids need to have time away from their devices. But for kids it's even more important because that break gives them the chance to discover what they're good at in the real world. Restoring shop, art, music, and home economics to schools would be a powerful way to give students these kinds of off-screen opportunities. Research has shown that some young adults who were addicted to video games stopped playing when they were introduced to fixing cars. Fixing real cars and real engines can often be more interesting than racing digital ones.

The Math Trap

When I first started high school, I was bored, and I did poorly. But when my science teacher gave me hands-on projects, it motivated me. Overnight, I became interested in science, and I started studying because I knew that studying was the pathway to becoming a scientist.

The hands-on experiences I had both on my aunt's ranch and with my science teacher helped me realize that I wanted to be a scientist who worked with animals. But I did not apply to veterinarian schools, which might have been an obvious choice for me, because they required applicants to have good grades in math, and I was lousy at algebra.

In elementary school, I was great at arithmetic. Addition, subtraction, and fractions made perfect sense to me because I could relate them back to real-world things. I connected fractions to cutting up a pizza, for example. When I grew up, knowing this practical math was extremely useful in my work designing livestock facilities. But algebra is where I hit a wall. Like a lot of object thinkers, I couldn't grasp abstract concepts, and algebra is all about abstract concepts. In high school, my teachers tried to pound the subject into me, but without images to visualize—without a pizza to picture—it was hopeless.

My editor for this book described her own similar experience with algebra. "I had a wonderful teacher who taught algebra using little plastic pieces and an image of a scale," she told me. "She asked us to use the plastic pieces to balance the sides of the scale the way we had to balance algebraic equations." This is a teacher who knew how to teach algebra using real-world, practical examples. (She should be put in charge of teaching teachers how to teach algebra!)

Since I never got the hang of algebra, I couldn't advance to college physics class. And since I couldn't take physics, I couldn't pursue engineering. And since I couldn't pursue engineering, I had to switch my major to a different science that didn't require algebra. The math trap caught me. I was screened out. What's crazy is that I'm often invited to consult at zoos when animals are acting strange, and I advise veterinarians even though I was screened out of becoming one.

Help Can Help

In college, I made sure to get tutoring immediately after I failed my first math quiz. For about two hours a week, my math professor took the time to help me better understand what was going on in class. In graduate school, I also needed help with math, so I paid a fellow student to tutor me in statistics. Without all that tutoring, I doubt I would have gotten through. In my job as a professor, I've noticed that the biggest mistake my students make is waiting too long before they ask for help. Help can help.

The math trap has only gotten worse in today's schools. The number of hours devoted to math has increased dramatically. Yet the number of students failing math has also gone up dramatically. More math gets taught, and less math gets learned. Failure at math became a common trend. If you say you're "bad at math," you're not alone. But it doesn't have to be this way.

This failure is specific to students here, in the United States, and the pattern becomes obvious every three years, when the PISA test is given. PISA stands for Program for International Student Assessment. It's an international test that fifteen-year-old students from countries all over the world participate in. The PISA is used to assess how successful different educational systems are at teaching reading, mathematics, and science. In 2018, kids from seventy-nine countries took the two-hour test. In the United States, 4,800 students from 215 schools took it.

Because it's an international test with many countries participating, the PISA is often described as the Olympics of education, and, sadly, the United States has yet to take the gold in math. If this were the Olympics, we wouldn't be awarded a silver or bronze medal either. In math, American students just don't measure up to their peers. (The country that did the best in 2018 was China. The United States was ranked twenty-fifth.)

So, every three years when the PISA math scores come out and everyone in the U.S. educational community sees how badly our scores compare to those in other countries, they decide, "We must teach more math!" And they teach more math. And test more math. And more students fail. It's a vicious cycle, and it's been the illogic of the past two decades.

Why Are We Bad at Math?

We're teaching the wrong math and we're teaching it the wrong way. As a visual thinker who has worked with a wide range of engineers, software developers, welders, CEOs, and other professionals, I understand that math is hugely important. But there are different kinds of math, and we should teach the kind that helps students succeed down the road in their careers. For example, California State University's entire system allows students to study statistics instead of algebra. Students in this program have been far more successful, and dropout rates are much lower than those who were required to take algebra.

Psychologist Jean Piaget.

Jean Piaget, a highly influential Swiss psychologist, is well known for studies

51 ▼

called the Conservation Tasks. These measured children's ability to understand concepts such as "same" and "not same" by showing them an image of two identical glasses. With these tests, he aimed to show the different stages of learning in children according to age as they develop logic and reasoning.

Do these glasses contain the same amount of water?

If the child agrees that the glasses contain the same amount of water, one will then be poured into a taller, skinnier glass. Piaget noted that children under the age of six generally concluded that the taller glass had more water. More advanced reasoning didn't happen until the children were over six years of age. He repeated this experiment with beads, rearranging the same number of beads in two different lines and asking if there were the same or a different number of beads. Again, the younger children had difficulty telling whether the number of beads changed with the new arrangement. I think these influential studies got us locked into ways about thinking how kids learn.

For instance, when researchers Margaret Donaldson and James McGarrigle devised a similar test, they added one key difference: a

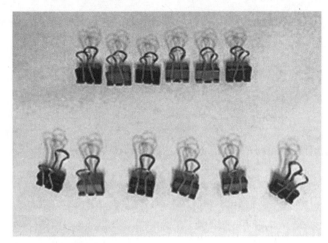

Six binder clips—or, in Piaget's experiment, beads—are placed close together in one row, with six spaced farther apart in a different row. Would you know, without counting, that the rows contain the same number of objects?

"naughty bear." The kids taking the test could now blame the bear for mixing up the objects.

The bear changed everything. Now that the children had a "real world" explanation for why the objects had moved, many more of them were able to come to the right answer. Fifty out of eighty got it right, instead of just thirteen out of eighty, as in Piaget's study.

How we learn is just as important as *what* we learn. Donaldson found that kindergartners and first graders are happy and excited to learn, but by high school they are often bored and unresponsive. "How is it that something that starts off so well regularly ends up so badly?" she asked. A New York principal was quoted in a 2014 *New York Times* article as saying, "I fear that they are creating a generation of young students who are learning to hate mathematics."

There are lots of creative ways to teach math. Nearly any sport or game can be used to teach math, too. Scoring can be used to talk about addition; statistics can be used to evaluate a team's odds, as well as individual performances. In basketball, every successful dunk into the basket gets two points, so it's a great way to connect kids with the 2 times table. Educators can use baseball to teach statistics by analyzing the odds that a player will hit a home run or strike out. For kids who prefer indoor games, chess is another game that teaches multiple math lessons. Imagine a class of elementary students playing chess for almost a year and then getting tested in math. That's exactly what researcher Michael Rosholm and his colleagues did when they replaced one out of four weekly math classes with chess instruction for 482 students in first through third grade. On average, the students who studied chess improved their math scores.

Then there are some kids who *do* get—and love—abstract algebra. But because our educational system assumes that all students develop at the same rate, we often don't let these kids advance. If a kid shows that they can do the next math level earlier than their peers? They are often held back. I speculate that innovators like Bill Gates, Steve Jobs, Mark Zuckerberg, and Elon Musk all dropped out of college or graduate programs because their classes weren't challenging enough. Just as we are screening out kids who can't do the math, I worry that we're also screening out the kids who *can* do the math (and other subjects) because we're not advancing them to their potential. We need to let kids follow their strengths.

A Hidden Figure

As a little girl, Katherine Johnson loved everything about numbers and math. She was a mathematical visual spatial thinker who thought in patterns. Fortunately, her elementary teachers recognized her extraordinary abilities, and they let her skip grades and start high school at just ten years old. She went on to graduate college, with honors, by age eighteen.

Johnson's genius was put to the test when she started working at NASA in the 1950s. Overt racism and sexism were pervasive at the time, and women were referred to as "computers who wore skirts." Black employees like her were segregated, and legally expected to use separate bathrooms. Yet Johnson's orbital calculations made the first crewed spaceflights possible. Astronaut John Glenn personally asked that Johnson verify the

Katherine Johnson hand calculated the orbital paths and the reentry trajectories for the earliest space flights.

computer's orbital calculations. It was her genius that enabled the safe return of the Mercury and Apollo astronauts.

If Johnson had been held back like many brilliant students are today, I wonder if our progress into space would have been held back, too.

If you look at any group of kids, it's obvious that they are not a group of clones or robots. Each one is different and unique. Each one has their own way of thinking and learning. Yet our educational system acts like they are all the same. We teach everyone the same way and test everyone the same way, with standardized tests. If the student doesn't fit the mold? Too bad.

In 1983, developmental psychologist Howard Gardner published his influential book *Frames of Mind: The Theory of Multiple Intelligences*. In it, he describes how no two people have the same intelligence, even twins. Gardner defined seven categories of intelligence: musical, logical-mathematical, linguistic, spatial, interpersonal, intrapersonal, and kinesthetic (a person's awareness of how their body moves in space). "It is of the utmost importance that we recognize and nurture all of the varied human intelligences," he said. "Even if you insist on teaching algebra," he points out, "algebra can be taught three or even thirty ways." Gardner showed that our educational system fails to recognize different types of intelligence. "How to educate individuals so that each develops his or her potential to the fullest is still largely a mystery," he wrote in a later book titled *Multiple Intelligences*. "We cannot afford to waste any more minds."

One Size Does Not Fit All

When I was eight years old, I still hadn't learned to read. My school's typical books just weren't working for me. My mother chose to teach me to read at home. Every afternoon after school, she would have me "sound out" syllables. Instead of *Dick and Jane*, we read *The Wonderful Wizard of Oz*. She would read a page of the book and then stop in the middle of an exciting part. Once, she stopped right when Dorothy met the Wicked Witch for the first time! It was agony waiting to see what would happen to Dorothy and her friends. Wanting to know what happened next highly motivated me like nothing else had. But before we continued the story, she insisted that I sound out every letter of the alphabet that she had taped to the wall. Then she had me sound out a word, then two words, then three, and so on until I finally got to hear how Dorothy outsmarted the Wicked Witch. As our lessons went on, she would read less and less, and I would read more and more, until eventually I was reading full sentences. One-on-one tutoring, and my mother's instinct to choose stories that kept my attention, worked. Within a few months of her taking on teaching me to read, I jumped from not being able to sound out a single word to reading at a sixth-grade level. Without this intervention, I would have totally failed in school.

Yet by the time I was in ninth grade, my writing ability was better than many of my current graduate students'. I can organize my thoughts clearly and clearly explain difficult concepts. My writing skills are what helped me get my first articles published, and those articles are what got me jobs. Over the course of my career, I've written more than one hundred scientific journal articles and fourteen books, three on my own and the others with co-writers.

Many of my students—even those working on advanced degrees—are unable to write their research papers clearly, and I often help them with things as basic as simple grammar. When I first noticed this, I was shocked. I asked several of my students why they found writing so challenging. They explained that they had rarely been asked to write a paper in school, and the couple of times they had, their teachers had never given them comments on their writing. It occurred to me that their writing couldn't be tested on a standardized test, so it was never considered a priority. This is clearly not acceptable. In any profession, a person must be able to explain things clearly in writing. Our educators need to put more emphasis on real-world skills like writing and less on testing. If they do, everyone will be far better off. The focus on testing alone is a trap.

The Testing Trap

Being good at taking tests has become so important in the educational system that some people are doing whatever it takes to succeed. That includes cheating. In his book *The Testing Charade: Pretending to Make Schools Better*, Daniel Koretz reports on how teachers are pressured to get their students' tests scores up if they want to keep their jobs. Sometimes they pass that pressure on to their students. In response, every kind of cheating has been used to make sure scores are high. In extreme cases, students have hired impersonators to take their tests for them. Still others have bribed proctors to look the other way. Cheating is happening everywhere and often.

But if we're going to talk about tests, we need to talk about the most powerful and dreaded test of all: the SAT, or Scholastic Aptitude Test. The SAT came out in 1926 and was intended to help students and adults alike. Before the SAT, it was challenging for college admissions officers to compare students' achievements. Is an A+ from a science teacher in Kentucky better than a B+ from a different teacher in Miami? Maybe. Or maybe one is a generous grader and the other doesn't believe in giving A grades. Colleges couldn't account for these differences and that made judging applicants difficult. When the SAT came along and everyone across the country took the same test, it promised to level the playing field by assessing all students the same way.

But once the SAT was given so much power, and everyone knew that this one single test mattered more to colleges than anything else, everyone naturally started doing whatever they could to make sure they would score well on it. Families who can afford it hire special tutors to help their kids prepare. Students learn testing techniques, like how much time to spend on each question and how to strategically understand the instructions. They take practice tests over and over so that when it comes time for them to take the real test, they have a huge advantage. Parents are willing to spend the money to help their kids succeed, and today the test-prepping industry has ballooned into a $1.1 billion business.

People of color are disproportionately less able to afford to pay for tutors and, therefore, start with an unfair disadvantage. It's part of the systematic bias in our schools and educational system. Because of this imbalance, the SAT doesn't end up truly testing kids' abilities; it favors those who can afford tutoring and extra help.

A study by researchers Steffen M. Iversen and Christine J. Larson compared test-taking skills with real-life skills. First, they gave college students a standardized math test. Some scored high on it, and others low. Then they asked the same students to look at information about a group of handball players and select the best ones. The results were remarkable. The students who scored low on the tests were better able to pick the best handball players. Their thinking was more flexible, while the high test scorers were wedded to a rigid approach.

It's clear that doing well on tests can get you into good colleges; it's not clear that doing well on tests leads to success in life. To thrive in life or at a job, you need to have qualities that a test can't measure: resilience, creativity, working well with others, good communication skills, and work ethic.

I still credit the time I spent taking care of the horses at my boarding school with helping me develop my strong work ethic. As I did in Mr. Patriarca's shop, I meticulously cleaned the work area (the stables), which was not a pretty job. I fed and groomed the horses, and my reward was getting to ride them. It was a big job for a teenager to handle every day. I didn't have the option of skipping a day if I was tired or needed more time for homework. It helped me develop my character and sense of responsibility, and I earned the trust of my teachers and headmaster. Most importantly, it allowed me to develop the real-life skills that helped me succeed in life more than any test I ever took.

There are people in my industry who run successful businesses with only a high school diploma, whose "real world" skills outstrip those of many people who did well on tests. People who hire staff to solve problems on ranches and feedlots have told me that a solid B+ student often performs better than a straight-A student, and I have observed the same.

Fortunately, the idea of using testing as the primary ticket to higher education is slowly changing. When more than five hundred colleges, including every Ivy League school, adopted "test optional" applications, the number of students who chose to apply skyrocketed. Students who once would have been screened out based on test scores now were given the opportunity to showcase their public service, hobbies, recommendations, and work experiences, and they seized it. This is progress, especially for visual thinkers.

The Label Trap

If someone asks me who I am, I say my name, and I add that I am a professor, a scientist, a livestock-industry designer, or an animal behavior specialist. Sometimes I just say one of them, other times all of them. But I never identify myself as someone with autism first. To me, my autism is secondary to who I am.

I credit my mother for that. It's possible that the most important thing my mother did for me was to see me as her child, not as her *autistic* child. Her belief that I could accomplish anything set me on the course for my life. It led to her making sure I had speech therapy, home tutoring, and supportive schools, which in turn led to my learning to read, write, and talk. I don't think I would have learned to do any of those things without her positive support.

Today, I meet loads of parents who identify as "disability moms" and "disability dads"at disability conferences, where I often lecture. They can't think outside the disability label. I suspect many of them have the same overall instincts my mother had, but the label gives them a sort of tunnel vision. I've also met eight-year-olds who, when they describe themselves, focus on their autism and tell me that they want to be autism advocates. (I tell them to go outside and play.)

In a book I co-wrote with Debra Moore, *Navigating Autism*, we called this mentality label locking. We define label locking as a focus on only the child's "disability" rather than the whole child. The concept of neurodiversity helps us see beyond "disability" and look at the whole child, strengths and challenges. Outside school, label locking can also keep kids from learning to be independent, like tying their own shoes, making a sandwich, or getting on a bus to go to school on their own. Instead of helping their kids learn these basic skills, some parents instead become "helicopters," who hover too much. As a result, they don't let their children learn from making mistakes as well as accomplishing tasks on their own.

One mom who had an autistic teenager started crying when I challenged her on this point. Her son, who was doing well in school, had never even bought a slice of pizza and a Coke on his own. It may not sound like much, but it requires communicating with a stranger, choosing his own food, paying for it, and doing the math if change is involved. It also teaches the value of money. Every week I was given an allowance and I had to weigh what I wanted more and what it cost: a glider or a comic book. And I also learned to save. This young man's mother admitted that she could not let go. Even though the attachment was well intended, the boy missed multiple opportunities to learn and grow. When parents seek my advice about their kids who are on the spectrum, I can tell by the way they ask their questions if they are snowplows, or people who tend to remove obstacles so their children don't experience any discomfort, or helicopters. Often, they will make excuses for their child's failures. My mother, in contrast, insisted that I learn proper manners, and she drilled them into me. By the time I was in elementary school, I had learned to sit at my granny's Sunday dinner without making a scene, wait patiently for my food at a restaurant without having a tantrum, and act respectfully at places like church and at the movies. I viewed all these as "grown-up" privileges. If I had a temper tantrum, Mother would take away my hour of television. Not getting to watch the newest episode of *Howdy Doody* was horrible and more than enough of a threat to keep me in line. (Back then there were no TV streaming services; if you missed the show, you missed it.)

For my mother, not trying was not okay. Once, when the neighborhood kids got together on their bikes to ride to the local Coca-Cola bottling plant, I begged my mother to drive me there. She refused. I'd have to learn to ride my own bike if I wanted to go. After trying and trying and skinning my knees and falling down a bunch of times, I learned! I was able to ride my bike. My mother had an innate sense of how far I could stretch without breaking.

Difficult as it was for me to learn these skills, mastering them helped me tremendously. Without them I would not have been able to forge a career path. This may sound basic, but kids, both neurotypical and neurodivergent, need to learn to be on time and be polite, neat, and clean. They need to learn manners, saying "please" and "thank you." As they get older, they need to learn how to work under deadlines and to execute tasks. All children need to be encouraged to be the best they can be, which includes pushing them to take on new life skills, even if it's difficult. Becoming independent is one of life's great rewards.

Throughout history, people with disabilities have been persecuted, marginalized, or kept on the sidelines. In the past, this was taken to extremes, and the treatment of people born with disabilities was shockingly atrocious. I get upset when I read about the cruel acts that humans have committed against disabled people, including starvation, abandonment, and chaining them up. Plato and Aristotle recommended infanticide for the disabled. People in the early U.S. colonies thought that mental illness was a punishment from God, and they often burned or hanged mentally ill people. The worst treatment of the developmentally disabled in more modern times was in Nazi

Germany, where thousands of disabled people were murdered. If I had been a three-year-old child in Nazi Germany, I would have been designated as "useless," and a drain on society, and killed.

Fortunately, within my own lifetime there has been tremendous progress in civil rights for people with disabilities. In 1990, two groundbreaking laws called the Individuals with Disabilities Education Act (IDEA) and Section 504 of the Rehabilitation Act were passed in the United States. The first specifies that an individual with a disability has a right to be educated in the "least restrictive environment" and be mainstreamed (to the extent possible) into classrooms with nondisabled children. These laws opened the doors of the public school system to students with diagnoses of autism, attention-deficit/ hyperactivity disorder (ADHD), the reading-based learning disability dyslexia, physical disabilities, and many other conditions.

Learning to Fail Successfully

I like to collect stories of people who have overcome adversity. They affirm my deep belief that hard work and independent thinking can pave the way for true discovery. Researcher Kelly Lambert, in testing rats, made a remarkable discovery. In her study, the rats that had to work and dig to find sugary treats were more resilient when confronted with new problems. The rats that were just given the treats and didn't have to work for them would give up more quickly when faced with difficult tasks.

When Theodor Seuss Geisel submitted his first children's book for publication, it was rejected by dozens of publishers. He was on the verge of giving up and burning the manuscript when it was finally accepted. We know him as Dr. Seuss, the author of over sixty classic books, including my favorite, *Horton Hears a Who!* J. K. Rowling, the author of the Harry Potter series, was also rejected many times before a publisher finally took a chance on *Harry Potter and the Sorcerer's Stone*, the first book that kicked off a successful franchise of beloved books, movies, theme parks, and a Broadway show. Imagine if either of these writers had been raised by helicopter parents. They would never have learned resilience, and we might never have had the chance to read about the Cat in the Hat or the Hogwarts School of Witchcraft and Wizardry.

Bob Williams, a Hubble telescope astronomer, also has a story of resilience. He had developed a theory that sections of the sky that astronomers had thought were empty might be worth exploring. He suggested pointing the telescope at parts of space where there was seemingly nothing to observe. It was 1995, and astronomers from all over the world wanted their share of using Hubble, and Williams's suggestion seemed like it would be a waste of the telescope's precious time. But as Williams explained, "I felt it had to be tried anyway. I told administrators that I would take full responsibility if it was a flop." He promised to resign from his job if they didn't find anything.

They pointed Hubble at a dark area of space near the Big Dipper and took a picture of it. The image that resulted surprised everyone. It showed not just stars but distant galaxies—more than three thousand of them. It was a major discovery, and today that picture, called the Hubble Deep Field, is considered one of the most important photographs of space taken in its time.

"If you're going to make a discovery, you're going to have to be a risk taker," Williams said. I would put it this way: in order to succeed, you have to be willing to try.

Bob Williams pointed the Hubble space telescope at nothing and found thousands of galaxies. This is an image that was taken later using the telescope.

In high school, my science teacher challenged me to make an Ames room, which is a structure that, by throwing off your perception, creates an illusion where two objects that appear to be two different sizes are the same. The project held my attention for over a month as I tried and failed again and again to arrive at the solution. Every time I didn't get it, I was frustrated. But I wanted to figure it out, so I would start over and try again. Finally, I solved it: the key to constructing the Ames room was to make the box a trapezoid rather than a simple square.

Eventually, I learned how to make an Ames room. But what I had *truly* learned was how to persevere even when I kept failing.

When I wanted to make some extra money in college, I thought I

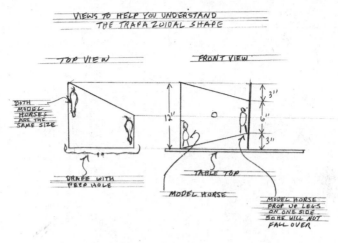

My schematics for an Ames illusion room.

could use my painting skills to make signs. When I first started showing examples of my work, I got a lot of rejections. That didn't feel great, and I could have easily given up. But because I had learned resilience, I kept going, kept improving my painting skills, until I finally got my first yes, and that led to others. I was paid to make signs for feedlots, thrift stores, and even the Arizona State Fair.

As an adult, I used these same skills when I showed prospective livestock clients my portfolio. I would lay my drawings on their desks and show them photos of completed projects. I called this the thirty-second wow.

People could not believe that my innovative methods would work. But today, my designs are recognized as the gold standard for cattle handling. All these experiences encouraged me to figure out how to do things for myself. They made me stronger and more resilient. That's a trait we need more than ever. Snowplow and helicopter parents take note: if you never fail, you never grow.

I see too many students give up on projects when they meet any resistance. In her bestseller *Grit*, Angela Duckworth defines "grit" as

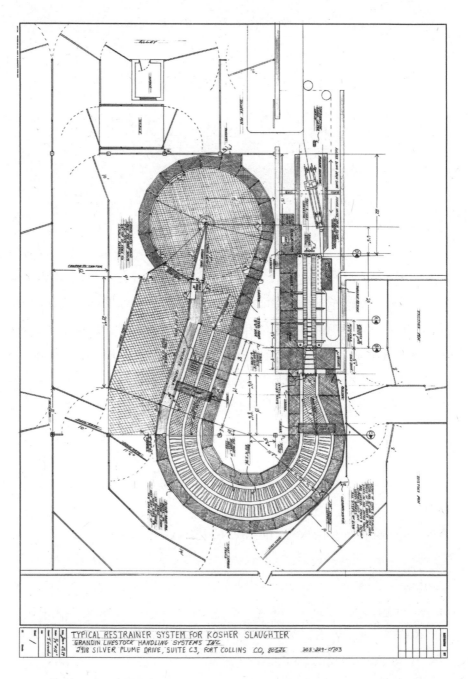

TYPICAL RESTRAINER SYSTEM FOR KOSHER SLAUGHTER
GRANDIN LIVESTOCK HANDLING SYSTEMS INC
2918 SILVER PLUME DRIVE, SUITE C3, FORT COLLINS CO, 80526   303-229-0703

I learned to sell my work by showing people a portfolio of drawings. This is one of my hand-drawn designs.

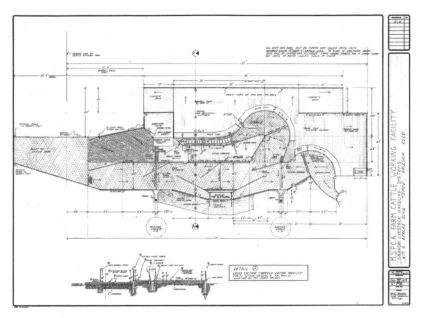

Curved cattle handling system I designed.

a quality that combines both passion and persistence to achieve a long-term goal.

One of my favorite anecdotes of resilience is about musician Stevie Wonder, who lost his sight shortly after he was born. In an interview, he describes climbing trees and running around with the neighborhood kids as a small child. His mother didn't let his blindness hold him back and keep him inside. He didn't get label locked. He also had hands-on experiences with many musical instruments from a very young age, and by age ten he had taught himself to play piano, drums, and harmonica. At church he sang in the choir. Stevie was told by some of the people at his school that all a blind person could do was make potholders. Through his perseverance and resilience, he did more than prove them wrong. He was inducted into the Rock and Roll Hall of Fame and is one of the bestselling and most beloved music artists of all time.

CHAPTER THREE
Clever Engineers

ONE OF MY FAVORITE TV SHOWS IS *AMERICAN NINJA WARRIOR*. It's not my favorite show because of the athletes (though they're amazing) but because of the incredible mechanisms in the obstacle courses. The unstable bridges, flying bars, warped climbing walls, and more are each brilliantly designed. Their complex moving parts fascinate me. I can tell that each of them was created by a person who is what I call a clever engineer.

To me, a clever engineer is someone who often works with their hands and comes up with mechanical solutions. Their experiences allow them to make firsthand observations about a problem and use that knowledge to solve it. Clever engineers work in every field; they can be clothing designers, artists, machinists, inventors, architects, or construction workers. Throughout history, clever engineers have invented new ways of doing things to help make life easier. Their ideas have helped civilization itself to grow and progress.

As a kid, I had a book about famous inventors, and most of the people featured in it were clever engineers, including the Wright brothers, who invented the first airplane (and ignited my lifelong interest in flying), and my hero Thomas Edison, who thought up hundreds of inventions. The modern-day patent system has helped many inventors like Edison protect their ideas from being stolen. The first patent in the U.S. was granted in 1790, and a special agency, called the Patent and Trademark Office, was created in 1836 to organize and approve all the new patents. Until the 1870s, an inventor seeking a patent was expected to send in a model of their invention when they applied to patent it. When I visited the patent office to give a talk, the first thing I saw, smack in the middle of the lobby, was an original model of a cannon from the 1800s. When I saw it, I geeked out. Inside its glass case, I could see its complicated parts, which had certainly been made by a clever engineer who could visualize how mechanisms work.

In its first hundred years of business, the patent office gave out patents for new inventions that impacted agriculture, chemistry, hydraulics, electricity, printing, paper manufacturing, bridges, guns, locks, you name it. It was a time of tremendous invention, motivated in part by the protection an inventor got from having a patent. The government, through the patent office, gives patents to inventions that are truly original. If your gadget gets a patent, no one else is allowed to use or copy your invention unless they pay you and get your permission. Patents protect inventors and their ideas. You can get a patent if you invent something new. Only now, instead of submitting a model of your invention, go to USPTO.gov and read about the guidelines and application process. In 1963, Robert Patch, age six, became the youngest patent holder in the United States, with a toy truck that could be assembled in lots of different ways.

Game Changers

- The printing press: Craftsman Johannes Gutenberg forever changed the printing process in 1436 when he figured out a way to speed up the process by using "movable" type instead of setting each letter one by one. His invention started the "information revolution" as books and pamphlets could now be printed and distributed widely.

A replica of the original Gutenberg printing press. It used a screw press that already existed to press the inked movable type onto the paper.

- The Colt pistol: The six-shooter pistol invented by Samuel Colt in 1831 had a revolving cylinder that was whittled out of wood. It automatically rotated the next bullet into position and allowed the gun to be fired multiple times before it needed to be reloaded. It changed the face of warfare as we know it.

- The telegraph: In 1837, Samuel Morse earned a patent for the electromagnetic telegraph, which changed the way we communicate forever and paved the way for methods we use today, like texting. His invention allowed users to send messages over long distances, using a system of dots and dashes that represented letters.
- Mechanical grain harvester: Robert McCormick Jr. invented the first practical wheat-harvesting machine. It replaced laborious hand harvesting of wheat.
- The car: Henry Ford didn't invent the car, but he introduced the assembly line in 1913, which accelerated the rate cars could be produced. This in turn made cars accessible to many more people—not just the rich.
- The internet: In 1983 Robert Kahn and Vinton Cerf developed a new way for computers to speak to one another.

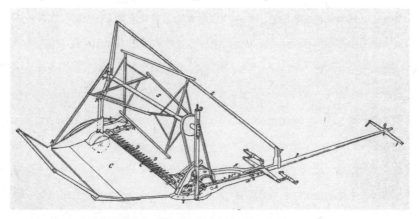

Sketch from an 1845 patent of a mechanical grain harvester by Cyrus Hall McCormick, son of the machine's inventor, Robert.

Just as movable type was responsible for the information revolution, their technology ignited the "digital revolution" that we too often take for granted today.

All of these inventions are remarkable and were likely created by object thinkers who could visualize and create their ideas. Members of my clever engineering department have transformed society.

The Little Guys

When I was starting out in my career, I believed that innovation typically happened inside large corporations. Instead, it's often the person "on the ground" who comes up with the big idea, who is involved with the day-to-day operations or has an intimate knowledge of the product or process. They are often unsung or don't get credited for their contribution. Hal Laning is one of these people. A computer scientist with degrees in chemical engineering and applied mathematics, Laning worked in a small, messy office at MIT. He had no interest in fame, he rarely published any scientific papers, and he spent most of his time by himself with his research.

As a young boy, Laning was obsessed with numbers. Every Sunday, the church in his neighborhood would list that week's hymns and their numbers on a sign outside. Laning would take those numbers and use them to make up math problems for himself. Laning developed a software program that used algebra to increase computer speed. It was instrumental to NASA's moon landing mission and allowed astronaut Neil Armstrong to control the lunar module. Laning's contribution was critical to Apollo 11's success.

I recently toured the workshop of a rocket scientist who designs the mechanisms that place satellites in outer space by launching them out of the tips of rockets This high-tech piece of machinery works on the same basic principle as the latch on your car's trunk. He also told me that he often goes to Home Depot to get ideas. He'll buy a pile of new tools, take them apart to see how they work, and apply what he's learned to his rocket projects. (We didn't have Home Depot when I was a kid, but I remember taking many trips to the hardware store, where I'd fiddle with every lock and latch.) Most of the mechanical inventions over the centuries were invented by hands-on visualizers who could see in their mind's eye how physical things could work. Where would we be without clever inventions that enabled the progress of civilization: wheels, tools, pulleys, bricks, and aqueducts? We don't think of these discoveries relating to rocket science, but all progress depends on the work of our first clever engineers.

"Quirky"

"Quirky" is the word used to describe people who don't exactly fit in. They are often socially awkward and intense. Elon Musk started his own company because none of the internet start-ups would hire him. He probably was too socially awkward for them. He describes how he sent his resume to Netscape (a search engine that was popular before Google) and hung around the Netscape lobby, hoping to talk to someone. But he was too shy at the time to approach anyone. Because of his experiences, Musk has said that when he looks for new people to work at his companies, resumes don't matter all that much to him. He doesn't care where you went to school or how well you scored on your tests. What he looks for is drive, curiosity, and creativity. He wants people who can make and fix things. I'd wager that a beautifully rendered mechanical drawing would impress him more than perfect test scores.

Where Are Our Clever Engineers?

America used to lead the world in manufacturing and making new products. But today, there are many countries who are better at both of those than we are. I think that's because, unlike other countries, we don't nurture our clever engineers. Despite this, there are still many U.S.-based companies that excel at highly specialized work. For example, the parachute that landed the Mars rover *Perseverance* so softly on Mars was sewn and assembled in the United States. However, the high-tech fabric in the parachute was made by a British company called Heathcoat Fabrics. Many U.S. companies who used to do these sorts of things have closed their machine workshops to save money. For example, when I first started working with meat companies, many of them had their own in-house manufacturing departments that invented and built lots of new equipment. But as people retired, they were not replaced, and the shops were dismantled. Instead of teaching the next generation of workers, their skills and knowledge were irretrievably lost.

This happened to the conveyor belt industry, too. The first conveyor belt was invented by the U.S. inventor Thomas Robins in 1896, and he started his own U.S.-based company making them. But his company is now owned by Dematic, a German company, and the U.S. is no longer a leader in the field. Dematic, in contrast to many companies in the U.S., has invested in developing a highly trained workforce that can create, install, and repair these machines. American companies like Amazon, Walmart, and Frito-Lay are their customers.

The parachute cloth for the Mars rover *Perseverance* was made in England. The rover took a selfie when it landed on Mars.

Other industries are led by countries outside the United States as well. The top manufacturers of industrial robots are Switzerland, Japan, and Germany. China, in addition to making most of the world's iPhones, also creates those clever machines that put the chocolate swirls into ice cream cones. Most startling to me is how much the computer chip field has been transformed. American inventors Jack Kilby and Robert Noyce created the first computer chips in 1961. Today, the field has grown exponentially, and the new computer-chip-making machines blow my mind. Each one is a huge rectangular box about the height of a bus. Inside, a maze of silver pipes both big and small connect to boxes, valves, and electronic devices that shoot out ultraviolet light beams that etch the circuit patterns onto the computer chips. They look like they came right out of Star Wars! But these amazing, futuristic devices were not created in the United States. They were invented and created by a Dutch company named ASML. How did this happen, when it was Americans who invented those first chips? Countries such as Germany and the Netherlands invest in their clever engineers.

Today, 64 percent of construction companies in the U.S. can't find qualified workers. When the beautiful new chemistry building was being built at Colorado State University, where I teach, the project manager told me that they could not find enough skilled electricians to hire to do the work. According to every report I've read, we are facing an unprecedented skills gap. European and Asian countries have trained and encouraged their clever engineers. We have screened ours out.

Where Ideas Come From

I couldn't have dreamed up my most well-known invention, the Hug Machine, had I not observed the cattle at my aunt's ranch. Watching how the cattle calmed down when they were squeezed on both sides helped me realize that I could design something that did the same for me. The Hug Machine calmed my anxiety and went on to help many others. My life would have gone in a completely different direction if not for the exposure I got from my aunt. Exposure to ideas, tools, and experiences at a young age can help young people launch their careers and their futures.

Having a hobby is a good start. About 50 percent of scientists who have won the Nobel Prize are more likely to have had a

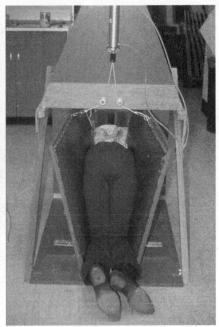

This was the final version of my Hug Machine. A front view and a rear view show how the air-operated controls worked.

creative hobby than other scientists. The curiosity that makes a good scientist also makes a good stargazer, computer programmer, or artist. Scientists who are at the top of their field often have diverse interests and are fascinated by many different subjects. Albert Einstein credited his hobby of playing the violin with helping him to formulate some of his most influential scientific theories. Inspiration can come when you least expect it, whether from books, museums, plays, or movies. When molecular biologist Angelika Amon was in high school, she saw an old black-and-white movie that showed chromosomes in a cell separating—she found it fascinating. Having always imagined that she would work in biology, she changed direction and pursued a career in cell genetics, becoming a top scientist in cancer research.

Apprenticeships

How would you feel about getting a free, high-level education and a guaranteed job after you graduate high school? Sounds like a good deal, doesn't it? That's what the Apprentice School in Newport News, Virginia, offers. The program teaches and hires apprentices in shipbuilding. Their students learn business, communications, drafting, mathematics, physics, and ship construction. It's not a typical college experience. Instead of desks and lecture halls, the classrooms are docks, a steel fabrication shop, and propulsion-shaft repair facilities. The graduates of these programs go on to design, build, and maintain ships for the U.S. Armed Forces. Government funding supports this apprenticeship program, just as it maintains the fitness of the fleet. Imagine if we did this for other industries, too. It's a model for how companies can mentor, grow, and retain the next generation of skilled workers.

Apprenticeships have been used for centuries to train skilled workers. Paul Revere, who famously rode to alert the colonial militia that British forces were advancing, learned to be a silversmith by apprenticing with his father. Benjamin Franklin, one of the writers of the Declaration of Independence, apprenticed at his older brother's printing shop. But the popularity of apprenticeships in the United States declined in the early twentieth century with the growth of public schools, and it continues to drop as more people choose to go to college after high school, instead of entering the workforce. Today, college is considered more important than, say, learning how to do electrical work from a master electrician. Working with your hands is, for some reason, considered less prestigious than careers that require academic degrees. But like most stigmas, there is no good reason for this thinking. While it's true that college graduates sometimes make more money than people who have graduated only from high school, there are lots of exceptions. Computer coders, lab technicians, industrial designers, and film editors are well paid, and these careers don't require a four-year college degree.

Finding an Apprenticeship

Looking for an apprenticeship? Check out this site: Apprenticeship .gov/apprenticeship-job-finder. According to Apprenticeship.gov, there are twenty-four thousand apprenticeship programs across the country in fields such as technology, fashion, environmental science, and more. When I looked up available apprenticeships in my home state of Colorado, one listing for an arborist jumped out at me. It described how the apprentice would learn tree biology, tree climbing, disease diagnosis, and tree trimming. I can think of at least two people I went to school with who couldn't sit still in class but would have loved to climb trees for a living. I also saw listings for apprenticeships in software development, roofing, manufacturing, utilities, hospitality, pipe fitting, and aerospace, to name a few. All were paid positions—apprentices don't work for free. I suspect that each of these jobs would be ideal for visual thinkers who may or may not have excelled in school.

These apprenticeships are a great start. But in a country as large as the U.S., it is not nearly enough. Other countries, such as Switzerland, have many more apprenticeships. Kids there can apply for an apprenticeship when they are as young as fourteen. They start the apprenticeship during high school, continue it after graduation, and eventually are offered a full-time job in the field. Their apprenticeships are designed to expose students to an adult work environment at a young age, teach them skills, and let them get paid while doing it. The designers of the Swiss program work closely with industries and make sure that the skills the apprentices are taught give them the real-life skills that are needed in the workplace. As *Forbes* described it, the Swiss apprenticeship model is "designed to fill the real needs of modern enterprises, which make them essential talent pools for some of the world's largest companies."

Italy's fashion industry provides another model. Italy has long been a center for fashion design, but they had a crisis when the number of new people with the skills to tailor their high-end clothing started shrinking. They created apprenticeships to address the problem. Francesco Pesci, the CEO of the Brioni fashion house, said, "Italy has always had excellent artisans and craftsmanship. We must invest in the training of young talent. We cannot allow for a generational gap." And Antonio De Matteis, from the Kiton fashion house, agreed: "Our breed of tailor was literally going extinct." The industry took stock of the fact that its highly skilled craftspeople were retiring or dying off and they pivoted. They created special schools to train the next generation of workers. These new apprentices have solved the shortage, and 100 percent of the students have gone on to careers in fashion. "It's the greatest investment we've ever made," De Matteis said.

In the U.S., we have an ideal that anyone can do anything. We want kids to keep their options open. We think apprenticeships may force a premature decision about the direction a person's life might take. But I fear that the opposite happens. Instead of keeping options open, we are closing them off by failing to teach real-life skills. It's not uncommon for recent high school or college graduates to feel the anxiety that the daughter of a friend of mine felt when she graduated: "But I don't know how to *do* anything!" she cried. Eventually, she found an apprenticeship of her own, working for a fabric artist, and she is now learning to upholster furniture. She is also pursuing her interest in the history and culture of textiles. Hopefully, this will give her the skills she needs to someday start her own fabric business. An apprenticeship in the textile industry might have prepared her better for the career she eventually pursued.

Every two years, students from around the world gather to compete in something called the WorldSkills Competition. It's like an Olympic Games, but instead of competing in gymnastics, hockey, and basketball, the athletes are skilled tradespeople and compete in vocational skills like fitting pipes and welding. There are always new skills added to keep up with the new technologies, and today's games include competitions in robotics, cloud computing, and cybersecurity. Switzerland always takes home the largest pile of gold medals. In 2019, out of roughly 521 skill sets tested, they won sixteen medals total, including five gold. I don't think it's a coincidence that the country with the model apprenticeship system is the one that brings home so many top medals year after year.

Inspired by the success of the Swiss apprenticeship program, Noel Ginsburg, a manufacturer based in Denver, has set out to try to replicate it here. Ginsburg corralled then Colorado governor John Hickenlooper to help support his effort. Hickenlooper was aware that while Colorado had the best economy and lowest unemployment rate in the U.S., it still needed more skilled workers in industries like construction, health care, tech, and "everything in between." Together, Ginsburg and Hickenlooper created a statewide apprenticeship system that gives students real-world experience and is helping close the state's skills and labor gap. Hopefully, more cities will follow Denver's model and consider making their own apprenticeship programs, too.

Internships

A cousin of the apprenticeship is the internship. The main difference between the two is that, historically, apprenticeships are paid and usually include the guarantee of a job at the end, while internships are often unpaid and do not guarantee a job.

Interns get to see how a workplace operates and how its day-to-day business runs. For example, interns at publishing houses get to learn the process of how a book is made, starting with the author's manuscript, going through the editing and design processes, which includes coming up with the jacket art. After that, the books are printed and shipped to a warehouse and eventually to bookstores. Interns might also learn how books are promoted and marketed, and how publishers use a combination of touring, media, and social media to get attention for their authors.

My writing partner interned at the publishing house Simon & Schuster, where interns rotated through various departments to learn about how the different parts of the company worked. As a highly verbal thinker, she gravitated toward editorial work. An internship helped chart the course of her career.

I tell kids all the time to try to take on an internship. If they are financially able, an unpaid internship may lead to a good job. Work experience is invaluable. It gives the student exposure to a field and the opportunity to gain practical knowledge of real-life expectations and responsibility. Interns can also make valuable contributions. One intern at a meat plant where I worked figured out why the electric pallet equipment for moving boxes kept running out of charge. The intern saved the day when he discovered that they were using the wrong charger.

Even if an internship doesn't lead to a job immediately, it will likely help you succeed in other ways. According to a 2020 article in *Fast Company*, students with internships on their résumé receive 14 percent more interviews when job hunting, and they get higher salaries. Employers like to hire students with internship experience; they feel that students who have completed internships or community service projects are better prepared for success on the job. There are lots of internship programs at a range of different companies. Some are very competitive and hard to get, such as at places like Google, Facebook, and Apple. Those are great and well paid, but the acceptance rate is minuscule. For instance, Google accepts 1,500 of the 40,000 applicants every year. (Your odds would be better if you started your own tech company, like Stanford dropouts Larry Page and Sergey Brin, who started Google.) But there are other internships out there, too.

Companies like IBM have internship programs that focus on data analytics, cybersecurity, and software engineering, which are great opportunities for spatial thinkers. Pilatus Business Aircraft in Broomfield, Colorado, has an apprenticeship based on the Swiss model. Their program allows students to rotate among departments to see what interests them. They leave the program with marketable skills and no debt. My co-writer first interned at DC Comics, the makers of Batman, Superman, and Wonder Woman. She got to meet the editors and learn all about how comics were made. She didn't get paid, but she learned a great deal about graphic art, and she got to bring home piles of free comic books.

Finding an Internship

Here are some practical tips for finding an internship:

Online listings: Job boards like LinkedIn, Idealist, and Monster .com list internships just like they do other jobs. Another website I love to recommend is called Handshake (JoinHandshake.com), which was founded by three students at Michigan Tech University. When you surf around Handshake, you are exposed to a wide variety of careers that you may not have known existed. The goal of Handshake is to help match companies with people looking for jobs and internships. Jason Aldrich, Georgia State University's assistant dean, reports that Handshake is "already helping to democratize access to more opportunities for everyone on campus, particularly our underrepresented minority students."

Job fairs: Some colleges and high schools host in-person job fairs, where companies looking to hire set up tables, and students walk around and talk to people about the work they do and what kinds of internships they have available. I have been to maker fairs and job fairs at which high school students have the chance to run construction equipment, learn about electric circuits, and program robots. This kind of exposure enables a student to "try on" a career. Historically, job fairs include companies in the consulting, financial services, health care, nonprofit, and tech industries.

Networking: It can work to ask your friends, family, and other people in your community if they know of any internship opportunities. Recently, I visited a major technology company and had the opportunity to talk to a young man from the Midwest who worked there. We were sitting in one of the company's trendy little cafés. I asked him how he had ended up in Silicon Valley, and he answered that one of his college professors knew someone at the company and had introduced him. That's good networking.

Creating your own internship: When I was in graduate school, I went to a cattle convention where I met the wife of a man who worked at a meat-packing plant. At the time, I was obsessed with learning everything about animals, and she offered to introduce me to her husband, who worked in the industry. The company didn't have a formal apprenticeship program, but they could sense my enthusiasm and created one for me. During that time, I took the opportunity to visit more than twenty different cattle feedlots in Arizona to observe their cattle, too. Watching the cattle during this self-created internship gave me exposure that led me to my eventual career in animal handling. Don't be shy. Sometimes people don't have the need for an intern when you ask, but they might refer you to someone who does. Make sure they know how to reach you in case an opportunity comes up later. Even if the job isn't exactly what you wanted, there is always something to learn, and it may lead to the next internship. The most important thing is to get your foot in the door.

Working Your Way Up

Besides internships and apprenticeships, there are other ways to succeed, too. Throughout my career, I have seen many examples of people who start on the bottom rung of a company and work their way up. At a large beef plant that I consulted for, I met a woman with limited experience who started out on the processing floor. The men working there didn't want to work with a woman and tried to get her to quit by giving her the absolute worst, dirtiest, messiest tasks they could think of. But she persevered, and within a few years she acquired the necessary skills and was promoted to crew manager, a position responsible for about a hundred people. Another man I know started out in his company's maintenance department, and now, fifteen years later, he oversees the building of its new plant addition, including the high-capacity cranes that lift huge concrete slabs. It is like playing with Legos but much, much bigger. In my own industry, I've observed technically adept people who started at the bottom work their way up on account of their mechanical skills, intelligence, and work ethic. And I know it's true in others as well.

Let's try an experiment. Imagine that something magical happened and—poof!—a fairy has turned me into an eighteen-year-old who has no high school diploma. My new eighteen-year-old self can't afford to take an unpaid internship. But the fairy has let me keep all of my seventy years of wisdom, so I know exactly what I would do. I would head straight to the largest company in town, with no money in my pocket but with big goals in my head. I would start at the bottom and work my way up. In many places, particularly rural areas, the best option is often a place like Amazon or Walmart. Therefore, I'd first try to get a job there or at Intel because Amazon and Walmart have programs that help their employees pay for classes that can lead to a GED (a high school diploma equivalency), and Intel, the multinational technology company, is working with different community colleges to create classes that lead to associate degrees and certificate programs in artificial intelligence. Ideally, I would try to work at Amazon because I'd love to someday work in their robotics or space-exploration divisions. I know this is possible because I talked to a parent whose child went from working an Amazon warehouse job to working in their rocket department by mingling with the rocket engineers in the cafeteria. Sometimes getting to the top floor means first getting your foot in the door and then climbing the stairs once you are inside.

Discovering Our Untapped Resources

Besides creating new opportunities through apprenticeships and internships, another way our society could create more skilled workers is by utilizing one of our untapped resources: people with disabilities who oftentimes have strong visual-thinking skills (as opposed to great social skills or verbal/writing skills).

Because visual thinkers think differently, their skills can be very valuable to a company. For example, when I visited Aspiritech, a website testing company, they told me a story about one of their clients. The client was losing 20 percent of their business, and no one could figure out why. After lots of investigation, they discovered the problem: the web designer had mixed up two digits of their phone number on the company website, which meant that potential clients were having trouble reaching them. That's never good for any business. An autistic employee who was a visual thinker was able to catch the error. Autistic people's skills at analyzing raw data and finding patterns within it is typically off the charts.

Other employees had reviewed the site many times, but it was this person's eye for minor details that was able to detect the problem. The website was fixed, and business started rolling in again. He had saved his company a lot of money. Yet, despite these remarkable skills, only 15 percent of people with autism have jobs. Since people with autism usually don't have the ability to make eye contact or engage in small talk, they often don't do well in interviews, which require both. Hiring managers need to understand that people with poor interviewing skills can still be an asset to a company.

The company Forest City Gear has also found ways to tap the skills of visual thinkers. They create highly intricate machinery for NASA, such as the tiny gears that rotate the cameras on the Mars rovers. Their work is highly meticulous and requires extraordinary attention to detail. Several years ago, Forest City Gear had a problem. They were having trouble finding enough skilled workers who could handle this detailed work. Ivan Rosenberg started a unique program to train autistic students. The twelve-week program combines classroom and hands-on learning, and teaches the skills needed at Forest City Gear. Now Forest City Gear has the skilled engineers it needs.

Similarly, Dan Burger, the inventor of Filtergraph, a computer program that analyzes large amounts of data collected by NASA telescopes, explains that people with autism "understand patterns in images at a superior level." Burger has been instrumental in creating a center for autism and innovation whose goal is to discover and identify such visual thinkers and set them up for long-term employment.

In corporate America, it's becoming more widely known that the talents that people with diverse minds bring to the workplace far outweigh the temporary inconvenience of the company learning how to reconfigure the workplace to accommodate the needs of these people. They are becoming appreciated for their deep knowledge, prolific memories, and attention to detail. Tech companies like Microsoft and financial companies such as Goldman Sachs are among those that recognize this and have implemented new hiring procedures to take it into account. Hopefully their initiatives will help pave the way for more.

Walgreens has also been a leader in this movement. Randy Lewis is the father of a disabled child and also a senior vice president at Walgreens. Because of his firsthand knowledge, he knew that people with disabilities could potentially be highly productive employees, with just some simple changes. He reconfigured the computers in two of Walgreens' warehouses so that using them required little reading. (Today, that would be called an accommodation.) This allowed employees who had an intellectual disability to do their jobs more easily. Later, when Walgreens compared the performance of their different warehouses to one another, they discovered that the ones with disabled employees outperformed the others.

Employees with autism have outperformed neurotypical employees at other companies, too. The Hewlett-Packard Enterprise

Company has found that if an autistic person is trained and given a few accommodations, like noise-canceling headphones and a quiet place to work, they regularly perform at a very high level, often more accurately than those without autism. And at Australia's Department of Human Services, autistic software testers were 30 percent more productive than their non-autistic counterparts.

Sometimes people who you would think couldn't be successful at a certain task because of their disability can surprise you. For example, you wouldn't think that a person with poor social skills and an inability to make good eye contact would be a good salesperson. When we think of salespeople, they usually have great verbal and social skills. But I recently met a socially awkward young man on the autism spectrum who proved the exception. He has an encyclopedic memory of every car's make and model, but because of his monosyllabic voice, his bosses assumed he would not be successful selling cars at their auto dealership. But the opposite proved true when they gave him a chance. As customers recognized his enthusiasm and depth of knowledge, his unconventional social skills didn't matter; they became a plus. People trusted him because of his unique directness, and, in the end, he made lots of sales. Perhaps they were also subconsciously picking up on this remarkable fact: people with autism tend to be exceptionally earnest and honest.

In researching this book, I went back and reviewed all the animal-handling projects I had worked on, and where I had spent extended periods of time on the job site and gotten to know the employees. The machinery designers and welders I worked with had either started their careers working on cars or they had taken a welding class in high school. One draftsperson had taken a single community college class in computer drafting. I'd say that, based on both their own self-reporting and my informal analysis, approximately 20 percent of the skilled people I encountered in these workplaces, whether diagnosed or not, were autistic, dyslexic, or had ADHD. All these amazingly skilled workers had some kind of disability, but they were given an opportunity to find their strengths and contribute. We need that to continue.

I think often of a field trip I went on in fourth grade to the Museum of Fine Arts in Boston. We were all fascinated by the mummies. As we made our way from room to room, from dynasty to dynasty, starting with the earliest and working our way up the timeline, I was surprised to see that the decorations on the heads of the pharaohs' cases became rougher and cruder instead of the other way around. I would have thought that things would get better as society progressed, not worse. When I asked our teacher why, she said something I've never forgotten: "Their civilization was falling apart." I still think of that when I see talent squandered or wasted, and when I meet kids who are "failing to launch." It upsets me. But internships and apprenticeships can be the rocket fuel that gets them going. They can give kids the skills and experience they need to succeed. They can also give them their first exposure to collaboration and working with others, which, as we will see in the next chapter, is often the key to innovation.

CHAPTER FOUR

Complementary Minds

THERE IS A ROMANTIC IDEA THAT DISCOVERIES HAPPEN WHEN A sole genius, laboring away in a basement lab, suddenly has a "Eureka!" moment—or breakthrough.

But that's not how it usually happens.

Throughout history, some of the most successful innovations have come about not through a single inventor working alone and having a blast of inspiration, but by pairs of people with complementary strengths working hard, hour after hour, bouncing ideas off one another.

Steve Jobs and Steve Wozniak created Apple; Paul McCartney and John Lennon wrote timeless songs for the Beatles; Marie Curie and Pierre Curie revolutionized science when they discovered the elements polonium and radium. Richard Rodgers and Oscar Hammerstein, two musical theater writers, created eleven musicals together and won thirty-five Tony awards for their work. Hewlett-Packard began in 1938 in a garage in Palo Alto (giving birth to the "Silicon Valley"—home to many of the countries' top technology companies) when two electrical engineering Stanford graduates created an audio oscillator used in animated movies. They went on to develop an entire line of audio instruments that led to innovations

TEMPLE GRANDIN

in printing and personal computing. The list of innovative pairs goes on and on. Collaboration is often the spark that ignites innovation. But it's not just any two people who can work together and set the world on fire with a brilliant invention. Usually, the most successful collaborations are the ones that happen between two different kinds of thinkers.

My grandfather's story of innovation illustrates this beautifully. His name was John C. Purves, and he was an MIT graduate and an engineer. He knew that the large airplane companies were struggling to create an autopilot system and that the approach they were using involved connecting the plane's steering system to a compass needle. But that approach wasn't working, because the needle was too shaky to be effective.

My grandfather decided to partner with Haig Antranikian, who had an idea for making an autopilot that didn't use a compass. Antranikian had suggested his idea to the airplane companies, but they were too stuck on the compass to consider it and had not taken him up on the idea. Antranikian's brilliant idea was going nowhere. Then he met my grandfather. My grandfather explained, "Antranikian had the concept, but he didn't know what to do with it. I saw how to make it work."

My grandfather, Antranikian, and two other men, Richie Marindin and Lennox F. Beach, set up a workshop in the loft of a trolley car repair shop. Together, the four men created a radical new technology. Building on Antranikian's idea, their device, the flux valve, was patented in 1945, with my grandfather listed as the lead author. He was ecstatic when the new autopilot system guided a plane on its first flight between major cities. My mother still recalls getting a phone call from him saying it was the happiest day of his life. This group was a prime example of great collaboration between a spatial thinker (my grandfather) and an object thinker (Antranikian). Their skills complemented each other.

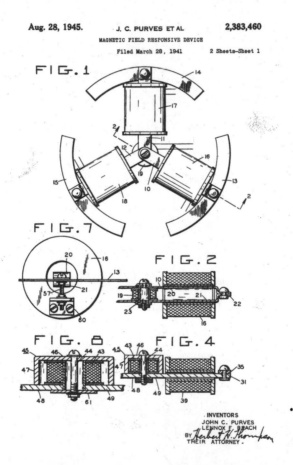

This flux valve was invented by my grandfather and Haig Antranikian, who was probably autistic. A stolen version of this invention was in every war plane during World War II.

According to my mother's memoir, *A Thorn in My Pocket*, my grandfather believed that original ideas come from "loners" like Antranikian. But without a collaborator like my grandfather, Antranikian probably would never have gotten his invention out of the basement and onto an airplane. My grandfather liked to say, somewhat judgmentally, that "original ideas did not come from company men, because company men all think in a similar way." They can develop, refine, and market an idea, but they cannot originate it. I think that's true.

Of the five major tech companies today, four started outside the corporate system. Steve Jobs and Steve Wozniak created Apple out of the Jobs family's garage. Sergey Brin and Larry Page met in university and later founded Google; and Mark Zuckerberg, who later dropped out of college, and Eduardo Saverin began Facebook in their college dorm room. Bill Gates and Paul Allen started working together in their high school computer class and went on to build Microsoft. For fun, they would connect their school's teletype machine (a device for sending and receiving telegraphs) and phone lines to the local GE mainframe computer and just mess around. The first program Gates wrote was a digital version of tic-tac-toe. Then he created a scheduling system for the school, a payroll program, and Traf-O-Data, a company that specialized in analyzing traffic. All this before graduating high school. When he grew up, Gates invented Microsoft Windows, the software that runs operating systems around the world.

Another pair of minds that made major innovations in the airplane industry were two brothers, Russell and Sigurd Varian. Sigurd was a thrill seeker who dropped out of college, reportedly due to boredom. (Jobs, Gates, and Zuckerberg also dropped out, by the way.) His brother Russell was his opposite. As a child, Russell was very shy and loved playing pranks. He also had autistic traits, dyslexia, and learning disabilities, which he struggled with into adulthood.

Together, they decided to create a new technology that could detect planes flying at night. According to the writer John Edwards in the magazine *Electronic Design*, "Relying on Russell's theoretical and technical knowledge, and Sigurd's mechanical abilities, they began developing plans for a device that could detect a signal bounced off an airplane several miles away." Using their complementary styles of thinking, they created a new instrument called the klystron tube. Today, it's known by a different name: radar. Without their invention, the Allies could not have won World War II.

Finding My Collaborators

When I was earning my master's degree, I first submitted my thesis idea about chute designs for cattle to two professors. According to my university, I needed to have two professors approve it in order to move forward. But those first two said no right away. They were very traditional in their thinking, and my idea was too "out there"; they didn't think it was a suitable academic research project. I could have quit and found another topic right then, but instead I decided to search for two other professors who would see the value in it and say yes. I was determined. I still remember some graffiti on the wall that had caught my eye in the university's art department. It read, "Obstacles are those frightful things you see when you take your eyes off the goal." The quote was unattributed, but it spurred me on. Later, I learned that it was said by Henry Ford, a fellow industrial designer and (likely) object thinker.

Foster Burton, a mechanical engineer, was the first professor I got to say yes. He didn't think my idea was crazy. On the contrary, he thought it was original and worth pursuing. Then Mike Nielsen, an industrial design professor, said yes too. I got the green light to pursue my thesis. Years later, I found an interesting video online discussing the differences between an industrial designer and a mechanical engineer. Industrial designers place a huge emphasis on art and drawing, while mechanical engineers calculate a product's functionality by looking at mathematics. The industrial designer creates the design, and an engineer makes it function. Nielsen and Burton were my first experience with this kind of pairing, but I would see these types of complementary minds pairing up again and again over the course of my career.

After I received my master's degree, I met Jim Uhl, a former Marine Corps captain, and my career took off. Jim sought me out after he had seen some of the drawings I had made while I was in graduate school. He was looking for designers for his new company and could see from my work that I was the kind of thinker he needed. At first, I was reluctant to take the job. I was fine with the design part of it, but Jim also wanted me to help him sell the designs to clients. Since I knew I wasn't a verbal person, this made me nervous. But Jim wasn't concerned. He valued the quality of my design work, and since I was the one who understood it best, he believed I should be the one explaining it to clients. I pushed myself out of my comfort zone and did it. The first time I went to a client meeting, I was very nervous. But I simply spread out my drawings on the table for the clients to review. I let my portfolio of drawings and photos of completed projects do the talking. And it worked.

I didn't know it at the time, but when I look back on my

collaboration with Jim, it is now obvious to me that Jim and I also had complementary minds. We approached problems differently. Jim was a verbal thinker. When he did a cost estimation on a job on a new plant, he would need to see everything laid out in a linear fashion. Then he would spend several days cataloging every gate hinge and several more nights crunching numbers. In contrast, I would estimate the cost of a new project by looking at historical data on the cost of previous projects. I was able to visualize the past projects and apply their numbers to the new projects, too. Both our approaches were accurate, and our collaborations were very successful. Neither one of us knew why we did things differently, but we accepted that we did.

Jim was a superb manager. He valued the input of different minds, and he had great skill in finding good people to work for him (including a young high school graduate named Mark Adams, who today is the vice president of Agro Construction). There was one talented young man that Jim hired who would do most of the construction on my dip vat projects. A dip vat is a narrow pool that cattle swim through to kill ticks and external parasites. I had the opportunity to design dip vats for six different feedlots because there was an outbreak of cattle scabies during the 1970s. The U.S. Department of Agriculture mandated that all cattle had to be dipped. The opportunity to design these systems helped to jump-start my career. The guy who constructed my dip vats was kind of wild, but even after he crashed a company truck, Jim told me he kept him on because he was talented. He also hired people from the local Native American community, as his construction office was located in Scottsdale, within the Salt River Pima–Maricopa Indian Community. Jim was an important mentor who helped get my career started. I don't know if I would have had the confidence to start my own company without his support. For ten years we did projects together, including the dip vat that is shown in the HBO movie based on my life.

After my partnership with Jim ended in 1980, I moved to Illinois to work on my PhD. I went on to work as a consultant.

I had many different types of clients. One time, I was brought in to help develop a new way of handling cattle in large beef-processing plants. The invention that resulted, called the center track conveyor system, is another example of how complementary minds work well together.

At animal plants, it's important to have effective systems to hold the cattle in a low-stress manner. Sometimes conveyor belts are used, similar to the kind at the checkout counter in the grocery store. But there was a problem with the design. The animals must be willing to walk in and ride the conveyor. The way it had been constructed in the lab, however, was just not practical for use in a real-life factory. I was invited to join the team and help rethink the design so it would function in the plant.

After analyzing the design for several weeks, I suddenly had a picture of the solution appear in my imagination. This is how my visual mind works. After I collect all the relevant information (more bottom-up thinking), a solution appears, fully formed in my head. The entrance needed a leg-positioning bar high enough to touch the animal's belly. This would induce the animal to straddle the moving conveyor. It also had mechanisms that could be adjusted for the size of the animal so that it would work for both small and large animals. I drew a design for it and shared it with the team. Now my work on the project was complete. My thinking-in-pictures mind had added the final pieces to the puzzle, and today the most widely adopted model for livestock handling uses my design.

The project wouldn't have succeeded without all the members on the team, including the guys in the shop who thought up the idea in the first place, the scientists who tested it, the welder who built it, and the visual thinker who innovated a new solution (that's me).

On every one of my projects, I rely on people with different types of skills to make it all work. I draw detailed plans, and other members of the team design the intricate mechanical equipment. They are usually object thinkers. Still others use their mathematical minds to come up with the structural specifications. They are usually spatial thinkers. Because we are collaborating and each using our own unique skills and ways of thinking, we can create large, complex stockyards and cattle-handling facilities.

Suits and Techies

I've seen collaborations fail on an epic scale. It usually happens when different types of minds have opposing perspectives or values regarding the task at hand. In some of the corporations where I've worked and consulted, the biggest divide has been between the "techies" and the "suits." A "techie" is a creative, hands-on person who is in the trenches, making the product. A "suit" is a corporate person in charge of managing the costs and profits. I'm a techie, but I've always gotten along with the suits. It's not that I always agree with them, but early on in my career I realized that the way for me to get things done was to be "project loyal." That means I care more about the success of the project than my ego. I will go the distance to get a project done right, and I am completely driven by project loyalty.

Projects self-destruct from an abundance of ego and a refusal to be open to opinions from other kinds of thinkers. At one plant I worked at, there was a "suit" who was inexperienced but had still been promoted from the sales department to head up construction. He was personable, highly verbal, and could talk people into anything. I'm sure that's a big part of how he got the job. Management wanted to cut costs, and he convinced them that he could slash the budget. But his ego kept him from hearing the advice of the techies on the job. They told him he needed to expand the wastewater treatment system, but he had promised the suits he could save money and refused to do the expansion. The system ended up overloaded. The city shut down the plant, and millions of dollars were lost.

Techies and suits are different kinds of thinkers. But they can still collaborate successfully. When one kind of mind respects and values other kinds of minds, things can work. But when it's the reverse and someone instead cares more about their own ego, things can fall apart.

Two Geeks Are Better than One

To design and construct a building, you need steel, brick, cables, wires, and more. You also need two different types of people: an architect and an engineer. The building can't go up without both.

Historically, those two people were one and the same. In the late Middle Ages, there was little division among the building trades. The person who imagined how the building should look was often the same person who built it with their hands. As building materials such as iron, steel, and reinforced concrete developed, construction became more specialized. Architects and engineers took on distinct roles. Generally speaking, architects are in charge of the grand artistic vision of a project, and engineers figure out the nuts and bolts of bringing that vision to life. Architects are often object thinkers who see their buildings in their mind's eye, while engineers are generally spatial thinkers who use mathematics to calculate the electrical systems, strength of the structure, and overall function.

Researchers David Cropley and James Kaufman studied the difference between architecture and engineering students by showing them pictures of different types of chairs and asking them to rate them by both beauty (how they looked) and function (how they worked). There were pictures of every kind of chair you can imagine, from a comfy beanbag chair that you could sit in to play video games to a metal desk chair that you might find in a classroom.

The study found that the engineers couldn't separate beauty from function. To them, if it worked, that meant it was beautiful. Beauty and function were the same thing. The architects, in contrast, differentiated between beauty and function. They were more likely to say, "This chair looks gorgeous. No one can sit on it, but it looks really cool." Interestingly, when I took the chair test, the chair I hated was an outdoor summer chair molded of curved plywood. It looked uncomfortable to me. But when I looked it up online, I discovered that it's on display at the Museum of Modern Art, considered by many to be a beautiful object.

Interestingly, the ways that architecture and engineering are taught in school also highlight the differences between these two ways of thinking. Engineering classrooms typically consist of rows of desks,

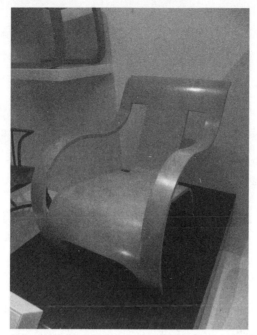

A chair I hated, on display at the Museum of Modern Art.

but architecture classes have students seated around large worktables, with art and drawings tacked to the walls. The curriculums are different, too. Engineers learn how to solve one technical problem after the other, in a clear progression, while the typical architecture curriculum is more open ended and emphasizes creativity.

When these two types of brains collaborate with one another, remarkable things can happen. When the 1889 world's fair was announced, France held a competition for architects and engineers to submit proposals for a building that would represent their country at the fair. The team of Gustave Eiffel and Stephen Sauvestre won with their unprecedented tower of steel, which used cutting-edge building technologies of the time. They went on to create a structure that is one of the most popular tourist attractions in the world, the Eiffel Tower. While one field couldn't exist without the other, architects generally get the attention and credit for their aesthetically daring buildings, so the tower was named after Eiffel. The object thinker (Eiffel) and the spatial thinker (Sauvestre) came together to create a brilliant building that continues to attract more than seven million tourists from all over the world each year.

NASA vs. Musk

When you just have one type of thinker on a project, it can show. A good example of this is something that happened at NASA. I've mentioned that I'm a NASA geek. One of the things I've noticed is that everything on the NASA space station is purely functional. There is no attempt to make it look pretty. NASA is not interested in pretty. Its space station almost looks like a junkyard, with monitors, wires, cables, plugs, and panels all in a jumble. It's clear to me that the space station was designed by engineers who are strictly spatial thinkers.

Elon Musk had a different vision for his SpaceX Crew Dragon capsule. I watched every minute of the broadcast and knew from the minute I saw the jet bridge that we weren't in NASA-land anymore. We were in another universe. While NASA's jet bridge looks like construction scaffolding, Musk's bridge to the Crew Dragon capsule looks like a sci-fi movie set: sleek and futuristic. NASA uses helmet designs like those of fighter pilots; Musk's helmets were inspired by the music group Daft Punk, and the spacesuits were designed by the same designer who created the uniforms for many of the Marvel Universe heroes. Musk's vision combined visual and spatial thinking—or another way to look at it: the marriage of form and function. I speculate that Musk's right-hand person, COO (chief operation officer) Gwynee Shotwell, was integral in implementing Musk's vision. She runs the day-to-day operations at SpaceX. She has a bachelor's degree in mechanical engineering and a master's in applied mathematics. She's inspired by Musk's vision, but what she loves is to make the rockets run on time. She's the Sauvestre to his Eiffel.

Jobs and Woz (or the Two Steves)

Another groundbreaking duo that created brilliant innovations was Steve Jobs and Steve Wozniak. Jobs was known for his passion for good design and beauty. His razor-sharp focus led to the beautifully designed Apple computers. But it began, strangely enough, in a low-tech calligraphy class that he took at Reed College. He described the typeface fonts and techniques he learned there as "beautiful, historical, artistically subtle in a way that science can't capture, and I found it fascinating." Jobs's visual mind cared about every detail, including the typeface. The next time you type something on a computer, have a look at the font list. You'll probably find dozens of choices there. That's because when Steve Jobs was inventing his first computers, he made sure to include them.

To make a beautiful computer functional, there needs to be a techie. Enter Steve Wozniak, the spatial thinker. He was the perfect partner for Jobs. Wozniak wrote in his book that all he wanted to do was design circuits and "come up with clever ideas and apply them." Walter Isaacson writes of their collaboration, "Jobs had a bravado that . . . could be charismatic, even mesmerizing. Wozniak, in contrast, was shy and socially awkward, which made him seem childishly sweet." Isaacson goes on to quote Jobs on the partnership: "Woz is very bright in some areas, but he's almost like a savant, since he was so stunted when it came to dealing with people he didn't know. We were a good pair."

Steve Jobs insisted that computers should look nice and be simple to use.

Jobs's interest in design combined with Wozniak's focus on function resulted in some of the most civilization-changing devices of our time: the Apple computer, the iPod, and, eventually, the iPhone, which users gush over. People still wait in long lines for the chance to buy the newest version of it as soon as it is released.

Once again, two geeks are better than one.

Communicate to Collaborate

I have a close colleague who specializes in creating meat-cutting saws and other high-end equipment. He is wildly successful and sells his products all around the world. He flew me out in his corporate jet to visit his factory. When I arrived, we went right to his machine shop so he could show me his latest innovations. There was no cup of coffee, no "Hi, how's the family?" or other pleasantries. He just wanted me to share my thoughts on his work, and that's what I wanted, too. Our minds were in alignment. We cared about the same things, so we didn't need any of the typical social glue or chitchat to have an enjoyable visit.

It's comfortable and easy to work with like-minded people who share the same interests and work ethic. But when different types of minds collaborate, their work can have far more impact. Researcher Anita Williams Woolley tested this idea by challenging one hundred sets of partners to play a video game that involved completing a maze and catching small creatures Woolley called greebles. When Woolley analyzed the results, she found that the teams that included two different types of thinkers outperformed teams composed of two similar types. The differences in their problem-solving approaches led them to have a better collaboration, and with better results.

When Betsy Lerner and I worked together on my memoir *Thinking in Pictures* more than twenty-five years ago, we had to find a way to tell my story. I'm a visual thinker, and Betsy lives in a world of words. My mind is associative, and I organize my thoughts by subject (the same way visual images group together in my mind). But to a verbal thinker like Betsy, these associations appeared random. She literally taped my pages to the wall and moved them around to organize my ideas into a user-friendly order. Her contribution was structural, creating a clear beginning, middle, and end, and finding words to describe my visual concepts. She also asked lots of questions, especially about things that are obvious to me. Together we found a way to merge my ideas and experience with her storytelling ability.

We've worked on many more books since then, including this one, and our different ways of thinking, mixed with willingness to stretch ourselves and be open to each other's way of thinking, makes our partnership work.

Making Music Together

The music I've loved since I was a child comes from musicals. I loved them then and I love them now. In high school, my roommate and I would listen to *Carousel* and *Bye Bye Birdie* and *Oklahoma!* over and over. I sang "The Farmer and the Cowman" from *Oklahoma!* in the talent show. And at my high school graduation, I recited the words to "You'll Never Walk Alone" from *Carousel*:

> When you walk through a storm hold your head up high
> And don't be afraid of the dark.
> At the end of a storm is a golden sky
> And the sweet, silver song of the lark.

It was a song that made me think about my future. There may be storms, but when you get through them, there will be a bright future. I have gone through many doors, and in walking through them I always come back to this song and the promise of a golden sky.

Composer Richard Rodgers and lyricist Oscar Hammerstein were the musical team behind many of my favorite musicals, including *Oklahoma!* and *Carousel*. They are another perfect example of complementary minds that created remarkable work. When they met, Rodgers already had a highly successful Broadway career. Hammerstein wasn't quite as successful but was

Complementary minds can create beauty.

widely respected. It wasn't common for theater people to start collaborating at midlife, but from the moment the two men decided to work together, something magical happened. In his book *The Sound of Their Music*, Frederick Nolan quotes Rodgers as saying, "What happened between Oscar and me was almost chemical. Put the right components together and an explosion takes place. Oscar and I hit it off from the day we started." *Oklahoma!* was their very first musical. Rodgers claims that within ten minutes of Hammerstein giving him the lyrics to the opening song, "Oh, What a Beautiful Mornin'," its unforgettable melody came to him. "When Oscar handed me the lyric and I read it for the first time, I was a little sick with joy because it was so lovely and right."

You can hear in these quotes the respect they had for each other's strengths and thinking. That kind of respect is the basis for true collaboration.

The two men didn't compose together in late-night, ashtray-filled sessions around the piano. Instead, Hammerstein wrote mostly from his home in Pennsylvania, and Rodgers largely composed from his home in Connecticut or his New York apartment. Hammerstein produced the lyrics first and sent them to Rodgers, who would then compose the melodies. In an interview on NPR's *Fresh Air*, Todd Purdum suggests that Rodgers and Hammerstein were never close friends. It didn't matter. Theirs was a creative collaboration and a business partnership. As Rodgers wrote in his memoir, "When a show works perfectly, it's because all the individual parts complement each other and fit together. No single element overshadows any other. It was a work created by many that gave the impression of having been created by one."

Different kinds of thinkers came together to make beautiful music together.

How to Collaborate

Since most people are very attached to the way they do things and how they see the world, it can be difficult to get different types of thinkers to work as a team. Here's one of the worst attempts that I ever heard. A large company wanted their employees to collaborate better, so they brought in a team of consultants and asked them to help foster communication between the people who worked in different departments. The consultants put the employees on teams and asked them to do absurd, nonpractical tasks, like design a parachute for an egg drop or do trust exercises in which you fall backward into someone's arms. These exercises only irritated the employees and made them feel less inspired to collaborate. What did an egg parachute have to do with getting their product to market more efficiently? How did it help them communicate better?

In my experience, the best way to encourage people to collaborate is to give them the time to learn each other's contribution to the big picture. I've found the best way to do this is to invite people from different divisions to shadow each other at work so they can better understand what the other does and its importance. Having each department offer a presentation to the other departments can accomplish this as well. This method can lead to a genuine meeting of the minds and better communication. An art director and a number cruncher basically live on different planets. I heard a story about a number cruncher who rejected an art director's request for a fancy printer that would allow the department to produce their own mock-ups of their ads instead of sending out their designs for printing. The cruncher had a budget to worry about, so it made sense to deny the request. But what happened was the opposite of the intended effect. Over the long term, printing the ads in-house on the expensive printers would have saved the company much more money than using outside printers.

A Collaboration That Reached the Stars

In 1965 NASA held a contest for companies to design the spacesuit that the astronauts would use in their Apollo program. They asked them to submit design proposals, and the company that designed the best suit would get the contract.

It was a difficult challenge. The suit had to be able to withstand the extreme temperatures of outer space. But just as daunting, the suits had to be flexible. "The gloves, said one official, should allow an astronaut to pick up a dime," explained an article in *Fast Company*. More than fifty years after the contest, CBS News reported that prototype designs submitted by the "big government contractors, like Litton Industries and Hamilton Standard, made stiff, bulky spacesuit prototypes that looked like a cross between Sir Galahad and Buzz Lightyear." Enter ILC, the parent company of bra and girdle maker Playtex. They weren't known for engineering, but the bra and girdle company had a hidden advantage. Undergarments (as they were known) need to be flexible, just like a spacesuit. According to the CBS report, "Each suit was comprised of 21 layers of gossamer-thin fabric, sewn to a precise tolerance of 1/64th of an inch." One woman confessed that she cried almost every night because she knew the astronauts' lives depended on her work. Now, that's project loyalty. Their design won the contract, and they began collaborating with NASA.

Still, the bra makers and the NASA engineers often clashed. The engineers wanted precise final drawings of the suits made before any sewing took place. But the ILC seamstresses didn't make final drawings. Instead, they used cardboard patterns, and sometimes they would make adjustments to the designs as they sewed. A seamstress told the NASA technical team, "It might look all right on that piece of paper, but I'm not going to sew that piece of paper." In this scenario, the NASA scientists were the suits, and the seamstresses were the techies, working with their hands, understanding the way things are made. They had to be nimble and think on their feet.

When the first astronauts walked on the moon, the public did not know that the spacesuit was made by bra and girdle maker Playtex. Playtex had the best design that was flexible.

It's also probable that the male engineers and macho atmosphere that pervaded NASA at the time made it difficult for them to show respect to a bra manufacturer and its female seamstresses. But the expertise and meticulous sewing skills of these women were exactly the skills needed to create the workable spacesuits. The seamstresses and the engineers both had to find ways to communicate and collaborate with one another. Fortunately, they did, and their contribution to the moon landing helped make it a success. Two totally different types of thinkers were complementary and mission-critical: scientists and seamstresses.

Thinking Outside the Box

In the 1970s, when the two Steves were working on the Apple II computer, they got into their first argument. Jobs wanted to make the computer simple and easy to use by providing only two ports, one for the printer and one for the modem. Wozniak wanted eight connector ports so the machine could be upgraded for future functions. Pure techie anticipating new applications. Jobs was convinced that for computers to become household appliances, they had to be less complex. He knew that, for most people, additional features just caused confusion and made the computer more difficult to use. He wanted to make a product you could take out of the box, plug in, and start using. He had a vision. Jobs won the argument, and because he did, Apple products are now pretty much everywhere. Would that have happened if Woz had won? We'll never know, but I suspect not.

During the first year of the COVID-19 pandemic, I lived almost exclusively online. I taught my college courses online and spoke at scientific conferences online. At first, many of my experiences with video conferencing were terrible. For one scientific conference, I had to go through an hour-long session on how to use a horrible program for logging on. Fortunately, engineer Eric Yuan thought about technology in a similar way as Jobs. When he was a head engineer for Cisco's popular Webex video conferencing platform, he could tell that the service was too cluttered and complicated for most users. He begged Cisco to let him simplify Webex, but they declined. I've seen a lot of companies fall into this trap. They resist change for the simple reason that they have always done things the same way. There is an expression, "Why fix it if it's not broken?" But resisting change can be a mistake because things are always changing. No one could have predicted the popularity of video conferencing: COVID accelerated the need and the demand. Yuan left Webex and started his own company, with a better, easier-to-use conferencing service. He made a new platform and billions of dollars. He called it Zoom.

I had a similar reaction back in 1998 when I tried out Google for the first time. When I saw its clean, white design and single box in the center of its page, I thought, "Wow, I can do this. There's nothing to learn." Many interfaces were just too complicated. The most superb, beautiful mathematical code is not going to be successful if the product is a cluttered mess that's difficult to use.

When I finally found Zoom, I was ecstatic. Finally, here was a service that allowed me to focus on my talks rather than the technology. This is why Zoom became one of the most popular virtual tools. It was simple, easy, and it worked. Eric Yuan strives to hire people who think for themselves and, like Jobs, believes that making the customer happy is the way to success. I think Jobs and Yuan are visionaries who can see and implement brilliant solutions. Then there is another kind of thinker altogether: the genius.

CHAPTER FIVE
Defining Genius

HISTORICALLY, MOZART, BEETHOVEN, DA VINCI, MICHELANGELO, Shakespeare, Newton, Curie, Kepler, Darwin, and Einstein are among the names usually associated with the word "genius." There is no shortage of biographies and books that attempt to explain what makes a genius. My first brush with one occurred in elementary school, when I was mesmerized by that book of famous inventors I mentioned earlier. I read it over and over, fascinated by the stories and inventions. From reading that book (and a lot of others, too), I've noticed some things that a lot of geniuses have in common. One is that, like me, many were branded "difficult children" by their teachers or parents. They were "strange." Some exhibited traits that we now associate with the autism spectrum and a variety of other conditions, such as hyperactivity (part of ADHD), dyslexia, poor performance in school, poor social skills, and an inability to focus. Interestingly, some with ADHD are also known as "hyper-focusers." This is when you are single-minded and can lose yourself in a single activity with extreme focus.

The Wright brothers made nearly a thousand test flights, obsessively studying and improving their flying machines, until they finally were able to achieve lift-off with the Kitty Hawk Flyer, the first successful flight of a powered aircraft, in 1903. These first flights—the longest of which covered 850 feet—would pave the way for the hours-long flights that are commonplace today. This speaks to me. I remember that as an eight-year-old, long after a "normal" or "neurotypical" child would have become bored, I'd adjust my paper airplanes over and over, experimenting with folding and refolding the paper to get them to fly that much better.

Bicycle mechanics invented the first airplane.

Like the Wright brothers, Edison was also considered a "difficult" child, and he did miserably in school. Edison himself said, "I used never to be able to get along at school. I don't know what it was, but I was always at the foot of the class . . . My father thought I was stupid, and at last I almost decided I must really be a dunce." Thinkers like Edison often become bored in classroom settings dominated by verbal education. These are the kids, as we discussed earlier, who need to be *doing* things. Autism was not yet a recognized term at the time, but from his own descriptions it sounds like Edison had some autistic traits. He had a big, dome-shaped head (larger heads are often a feature of autism), he memorized every street in his town, and he hammered people with questions.

After learning that a teacher had called Edison "addled," his mother, herself a former teacher, pulled him out of grade school and taught him herself, just like my mother did for me. She exposed him to a wide range of books, including Richard Green Parker's *A School Compendium of Natural and Experimental Philosophy*. This book included everything from the sixty-one known elements (today there are 118 known elements that make up the Periodic Table) to the six fundamental instruments: the pulley, the lever, the wedge, the screw, the inclined plane, and the wheel.

At twelve, Edison started working as a newsboy for the Grand Trunk Railroad. During that time, he taught himself several skills that would serve him well later in life. The first was business. As a newsboy, he not only sold papers but figured out how to make money selling groceries to train passengers, too. He wrote and printed his own mini newspaper using the content that he read off telegraph reports. He called it *The Weekly Herald* and sold it to passengers for three cents a copy. During that same period, Edison built a laboratory in his family's basement and constantly did experiments there. Unfortunately, one time when he tried doing an experiment on a train's baggage car, he accidentally set the car on fire.

In addition to his mother, Edison had two other mentors who helped shape his life. The first, James MacKenzie, was a telegraph officer and stationmaster who taught Edison how to use a telegraph machine. The second was Franklin Leonard Pope, who was an electrical engineer, inventor, and patent lawyer. Pope was instrumental in teaching Edison how to patent his inventions. We can see from Edison's story that his genius didn't happen in a vacuum. Edison benefited from mentors who helped him, and from early exposure to mechanical and electrical equipment. He also developed a strong work ethic as a vendor and newsboy.

The final clue for me that Edison was a visual thinker is this telling quote included in Frank Lewis Dyer and Thomas Commerford Martin's biography of him: "I can always hire some mathematicians, but they can't hire me." By his own admission, Edison's mechanical mind far outstripped his mathematical abilities. I believe he was an object thinker because of his abundance of curiosity combined with his tendency to make things. This type of thinking is probably what led him to fail at school, but it also helped him succeed as an inventor.

Another genius who did terribly in school was the great artist Michelangelo. His works are among the most remarkable of all time. They include the sculptures of *David* and *Moses* and the painted ceiling of the Sistine Chapel. As with Edison, Michelangelo left school at a young age, and he also later dropped out of a three-year apprenticeship after one year, claiming there was nothing left for him to learn. Like the Wright Brothers, he was also socially awkward, and he preferred working alone rather than with other artists. Because of this, some think that he too had autistic traits. According to Michelangelo's first biographer, Ascanio Condivi, "Passionate solitude was the soul and genius of Michelangelo." For much of his life, he lived alone and couldn't be bothered to bathe or to take his shoes off to go to bed. Poor hygiene is common in people on the autism spectrum, usually because the sensation of bathing can feel unpleasant to them.

As a young man, Michelangelo also had the benefit of two

mentors. The first was Domenico Ghirlandaio, to whom he was apprenticed at age thirteen. He exposed Michelangelo to the process of painting and drawing. A second mentor, Lorenzo de' Medici, who was a patron of the arts, took young Michelangelo into his home and provided an environment where his abilities could flourish. As journalist and author Eric Weiner observes, de' Medici deserves great credit for developing Michelangelo's talents. He spotted the work of a young "nobody" and "acted boldly to cultivate it."

Michelangelo also might have been one of these extremely rare minds that used both object and spatial thinking. He created two-dimensional paintings with photographic detail, like in the ceiling of the Sistine Chapel, but he also had the skills of a spatial thinker, which he used to create realistic three-dimensional sculptures such as *David*.

Albert Einstein is another genius who was "difficult." He didn't speak fluidly until age seven, and his sister once said, "He had such difficulty with language that those around him feared he would never learn." Like the other geniuses we have looked at, Einstein struggled in school, was socially awkward, and cared little for personal grooming. He had emotional outbursts and avoided eye contact. According to a biography by Walter Isaacson, he was "the patron saint of distracted school kids everywhere."

Even as an adult and professor, he refused to wear suits and ties and preferred soft, comfortable clothes. It's possible his aversion to suits and ties was a sensory issue. There is a lot of debate as to whether Albert Einstein had autistic traits. Einstein described how his mind worked: "Thoughts do not come in any verbal formulation. I rarely think in words at all." It is also reported that Einstein was surprised when he learned that other people think mainly in words. Neither his biographer Walter Isaacson nor the late Oliver Sacks, a famous neurologist, believed that Einstein had Asperger's, pointing to his ability to have close, lasting relationships as an adult. That isn't enough evidence for me; I've met many people with autism who are married or in relationships. But even so, Einstein still described himself as a loner: "I am truly a 'lone traveler' and have never belonged to my country, my home, my friends, or even my immediate family with my whole heart . . . I have never lost a sense of distance and a need for solitude."

What's interesting to me is that Einstein, as a scientist, and Michelangelo, as an artist, both excelled at spatial *and* object thinking. This is very rare. Perhaps this dual ability provides a new definition of genius.

Genius and Difference

Today, it's important for us to recognize that people who think differently are just that: different. Earlier we talked about the term "neurodiversity." It originated in the autism community, where it was a rallying cry for people who had been marginalized because of their differences. (Historically, people like me who had antisocial traits and little to no language as a child were placed in institutions.) This new vocabulary offers a way for people to discuss and think about differences, and it gives people on the spectrum a positive way to see themselves.

When I talk to autism groups, I like to share one of my favorite scientific papers by J. E. Reser, which looks at the ways that different

Lions live in social groups.

Leopards are solitary and share some characteristics with autistic people. Leopards and lions are examples of social differences in animals.

animals think and interact. Some animals are more social. Others are loners. Lions live in social groups, while male and female tigers and leopards are solitary except at mating time. Chimpanzees live within communities, while orangutans are solitary. Wolves live in packs. Striped hyenas live alone. So, if leopards or tigers were people, would they be diagnosed with autism on account of their antisocial behavior? Are they defective? Do leopards have a disorder? In the animal kingdom, we don't apply these labels. I don't think we should apply them to describe humans either.

Today, the term "neurodiversity" has been expanded beyond autism to include dyslexia, ADHD, sensory processing disorder, learning disabilities, hyperactivity, Tourette syndrome, OCD, bipolar disorder, schizophrenia, and other conditions. The idea being that these differences should be looked at as positive differences that sometimes might look like disabilities in one setting (like a classroom) but be an advantage in another (like the patent office). The conditions listed above, in small amounts, might provide an advantage in certain fields. Reporter Matt McFarland wrote in *The Washington Post*, while "full-blown Asperger's Syndrome or autism hold back careers, a smaller dose of associated traits appears critical to hatching innovations that change the world." And researcher Penny Spikins speculates that it may have been a Stone Age person with autism who had such exceptional attention to detail that they invented the bow and arrow and helped advance civilization.

The Beautiful Mind

John Nash was a person with schizophrenia who was also considered a genius. He earned his PhD at age twenty-two and went on to create what he called Nash equilibrium theory, a mathematical tool that can be used to predict how people will behave in certain situations. It's been used to advance thinking in many fields, including biology, politics, and philosophy. It was even used to develop the popular reality gameshow *Survivor*. Nash received a Nobel Prize in Economics for his contributions to game theory.

Nash did well in school, but he was also a loner and had a hard time making friends. He often spoke out of turn. This is something that I did and sometimes still do. Cutting people off can be interpreted as rude. But people on the spectrum can have difficulty with social cues. As he got older, Nash began to suffer from paranoid delusions and psychotic breakdowns, which he endured for the rest of his life. His story was retold in the movie *A Beautiful Mind*, which won the Oscar for Best Picture in 2002. The question remains: Was he a genius because of his schizophrenia? Or in spite of it?

A more current example of a difference that proved to be advantageous is the Deaf high school football team in California who played an undefeated season in 2002. Their coaches explained that the Deaf players "have heightened visual senses that make them alert to movement. And because they are so visual, deaf players have a more acute sense of where their opponents are on the field." The coaches also credited their success with the way the players communicated, through a "flurry of hand movements between each play." Unlike their hearing counterparts, the Deaf players could signal at great speed and with no time wasted. "They communicate better than any team I have ever coached against," reported a coach whose team the Deaf players beat. Their communication difference turned out to be an advantage on the field.

There are many people on the autism spectrum who work in tech. I interviewed one software engineer who fit the profile: he taught himself to program as a child, his single-minded focus sometimes frustrated others, and he performed poorly in school. Yet he is now a highly successful software engineer at a prestigious tech company. His intensity, a part of his autism, has helped him succeed. Peter Thiel, the co-founder of PayPal, has explained that in Silicon Valley many of the successful entrepreneurs are on the autism spectrum, which "happens to be a plus for innovative and great companies." Here, autism can be an advantage.

Many people believe that Mark Zuckerberg, the founder of Facebook, is on the autism spectrum as well. He has been described as robotic, socially awkward, and intensely single-minded. He wears a gray T-shirt almost every day, saying that he wants to focus his decision-making energy on Facebook, not fashion. It seems ironic that it took a person famous for having difficulty connecting with people to create a platform for everyone in the world to connect. Maybe that's the point. Maybe his autistic traits were an advantage for him, too.

Another unlikely person who captured the world's attention is a young autistic girl from Stockholm. You would think since Greta Thunberg has a monotone delivery and makes limited eye contact that she would not be able to transfix the world and motivate a new generation of climate activists. Yet she has. Thunberg describes her differences as her superpower.

Nature vs. Nurture

Scientists have been asking questions about human development for years. Why does one sibling in a family thrive and another does not? Why are some children in a family tall and others short? How does one family wind up with all musicians and another with all lawyers? How much of a person's abilities are biological and how much is learned? What goes into making a person the person they are?

You might have heard these questions boiled down to a single question: Is it *nature* or *nurture*? Sir Francis Galton was the first to use the term "nature versus nurture" and it still captures how we think about these deep questions. Galton was the first to use twin studies, and his work pointed the way for others to look at twins as well. However, he also used his findings to develop a theory called eugenics, which advanced the idea that some races and social classes were genetically superior to others. His theories have been used historically to oppress people, including by Adolf Hitler, who advanced the idea of a superior race of German people and tried to systematically eliminate Jewish people, disabled people, and many others who didn't conform to his ideal. The Holocaust is one of the most evil crimes against humanity in history. Galton's ideas have been thoroughly debunked in the scientific community.

Back in the 1940s through 1960s, autism was not considered genetic. Instead, the widely accepted theory was that it was *nurture* that caused autism, or, specifically, a mother's lack of warmth that caused her child to develop autism. These moms were nicknamed "refrigerator mothers" and blamed for "making" their children autistic. Many mothers suffered with guilt over this theory. Bernard Rimland, a research psychologist and the father of a son with autism, refuted this idea, however, and he eventually discovered that the source of autism is biological.

During our fetal development, we grow a huge pile of cells quickly, and this forms our brain's cerebral cortex. In addition to language, the cerebral cortex is responsible for sensory processing, intelligence, thought, memory, perception, motor function, and executive function—things that go into our personalities and make us who we are. The emotional systems located beneath the cerebral cortex also contribute to a person's personality. Emotions make us happy, sad, or angry. While growing a brain is an extremely complex process, most of the time it happens in a straightforward way, and most babies are born without complications. But sometimes, unusual factors can impact a brain's development.

To better understand genetic differences, psychologist Thomas Bouchard Jr., at the University of Minnesota, started studying 137 pairs of twins in 1979. He found that identical twins who were raised apart were as likely to share certain personality traits, interests, and attitudes as identical twins who were raised together. The findings led Bouchard to conclude that "every behavioral trait so far investigated turns out to be associated with genetic variation."

Researcher Örjan de Manzano also studied twins, comparing the brain scans of sets of twins, one of whom was taught to play the piano while the other was either relatively or completely unfamiliar with the instrument. The twins who had learned piano were found to have increased thickness in both the auditory cortex and the areas associated with motor control of the hands. Increased use of these parts of the brain evidently caused a physical increase in brain tissue. The piano lessons had made a physical difference in the brain.

Thomas Bouchard conducted an influential study of twins raised apart.

One way to illustrate these differences is to imagine two identical cars that are the same model, same make, same bells and whistles. They're almost exactly the same—just like identical twins. But each has its quirks. Perhaps a worker put more glue on one door seal, or tightened a single bolt a little more or less than another. These tiny differences, like cell mutations, will impact how the two cars come off the line, each one driving a little differently. That's how nurture can impact human brain development, too.

Even with all the twin studies that have been done, scientists still don't know why the exact same genetic trait can be a liability in one person and a gift in another. Take the case of Leslie Lemke. He became blind at six months old and has brain damage and cerebral palsy. This is why his parents were utterly shocked when they discovered him playing Tchaikovsky's Piano Concerto No. 1 on their family's piano when he was fourteen. He had only heard it once on the television. He could not read music and had never taken a piano lesson. Yet Lemke can play Tchaikovsky, and any other piece of music after hearing it. He was lucky to have a piano available to play.

Lemke went on to give concerts throughout his life and showcased his remarkable skills. And while he has trouble speaking, he can sing any song while playing. Some believe that in cases like Lemke's, an abnormality in the brain shuts the left hemisphere and allows for greater activity on the right. It's as if there is no balance between the two hemispheres, and so the right hemisphere barrels on without any brakes or stopgaps, reaching extraordinary levels of mastery. But why did this give Lemke the gift to play classical piano, while others with the same condition can't carry a tune? We still don't know.

An MRI of a brain will show the pathways in the brain that process language. In an MRI of my brain, it showed that I had narrower "streets" for speaking, which explained why speech came late in my life and with much difficulty. My speech developed, or you could say my streets widened, because of my mother's nurturing and the interventions she took, such as hiring nannies and tutors who worked with me.

Genius and Dyslexia

Film director Steven Spielberg is one of the greatest film directors of all time. His body of work includes *Jaws, Raiders of the Lost Ark, E.T. the Extra-Terrestrial, Jurassic Park*, and *Schindler's List*. He is often held up as a genius filmmaker—and like many other geniuses we've looked at, he struggled in school. His teachers believed that he was not trying hard enough. He was also often bullied for being different. But he was exposed to filmmaking early. His family had a movie camera and let Spielberg use it. First, he filmed family gatherings; then, at age twelve, he made his first movie. By age eighteen, he had made a full-length movie titled *Firelight* for less than $600. It was about aliens, a theme he would return to in *E.T.*, which is about accepting individuals who are different. Finally, at age sixty, after he had enjoyed much success, Spielberg was diagnosed with dyslexia, a syndrome where people have difficulty reading. It makes putting letters and words in order challenging and is associated with greater activity in the right frontal lobe, the area that is also the home of spatial visualizing. In other words, it's possible that the very part of the brain that made Spielberg dyslexic also made him a visual genius.

Another artist considered to be a genius who likely had dyslexia was Pablo Picasso. A co-founder of the early twentieth-century Cubist movement in painting, Picasso's art is known for breaking down scenes and portraits into abstractions with powerful emotional impact. In his book *Creating Minds*, Howard Gardner notes that Picasso had "precocious spatial intelligence but very meager scholastic intelligence," which can be translated as very smart but bad at school. My favorite observation about him comes from Picasso's friend, the writer Gertrude Stein, who said: "Picasso wrote painting as other children wrote their abc's. Drawing always was his only way of talking."

There are many successful people with dyslexia in business and other creative endeavors. British entrepreneur Sir Richard Branson owns over four hundred companies, including the airline he founded, Virgin. Celebrity chef Jamie Oliver and entertainer Whoopi Goldberg have talked about their dyslexia publicly. Ingvar Kamprad, the Swedish founder of IKEA, organized his giant furniture chain store using a naming system that he could easily visualize and that was easier to deal with than a numerical system. He gave furniture all kinds of names including his favorite places, which is why you might find a sofa called Extop, named for a Stockholm suburb, or a trash can called Bolmen after a lake in southern Sweden.

By third grade, Ari Emanuel, CEO of the talent agency Endeavor, was still unable to read and was diagnosed with dyslexia and ADHD. He was bullied, too. When he received an award from the Lab School in Washington, DC, which specializes in learning disabilities, he said in his speech that dyslexia was a gift that can give people "the insight to find inventive solutions to life—and in business—that others, when they're in those situations, probably never find."

Genius and Math

Most excellent coders and software developers have at least two things in common. First, that they gravitated toward math at an early age, and second, that they are excellent at pattern recognition. They can "see" the repeating details in the numbers. This is the visual-spatial, mathematical mind. Alan Turing, who is widely credited with inventing the first modern computer, thought this way.

Turing's mathematical abilities were apparent when he was very young. As a boy, he would study the serial numbers on the lampposts in his neighborhood. By the time he was sixteen, he was doing advanced, highly complicated math, even though he had never studied it in school. It's possible that Turing may have been introduced to these complex ideas by Einstein's book on the theory of relativity, which his grandfather had given him as a gift. His headmaster and his teachers thought he was a difficult student, and they criticized him for being dirty and sloppy. (A trait we've seen in Michelangelo and Einstein.) After he graduated high school, he went on to study advanced math and cryptology at King's College in Cambridge. Thanks to the mentorship of two professors who encouraged his math skills, Turing received his PhD and produced work in mathematical biology, explaining things as varied as how zebras get their stripes and making groundbreaking advancements in computing.

When World War II broke out, Turing's life took a sharp turn. During World War II, both sides used codes to send messages to their soldiers. By coding their messages, each side hoped to ensure that if their enemy captured a message, it wouldn't give away crucial information. The Germans used something called the Enigma machine to encrypt their messages. Using a prototype computer that he invented, Turing, on behalf of Britain and the Allied forces, was able to detect the patterns within the Germans' code and break it. Cracking the code made it possible for the British to anticipate Germany's plans. Once Turing broke their code, Germany could no longer successfully plan any surprise attacks. It wouldn't be a stretch to say that Turing's spatial thinking paved the way for the Allied victory in World War II and saved the free world.

The Enigma machine was used by the Germans during World War II to send secret military commands to their ships. The brilliant mathematician Alan Turing deciphered their code, which helped the allies win World War II.

Tragically, Turing's career and unparalleled contributions abruptly ended at age forty-one. He was found guilty of being gay, which was a crime in Britain at the time. He was forced by court order to take estrogen, which they thought would suppress his sexual orientation.

He took his own life in 1954. As I write this, I get very upset at this tragic ending to a brilliant mind and hero.

Musk is another genius who gravitated toward math at an early age. When he was just ten years old, he taught himself to code, and at age twelve, he designed a video game called Blastar. In Blastar, the opening screen told players that they had to "destroy [the] alien freighter carrying deadly hydrogen bombs." By today's gaming standards, Blastar would seem kind of basic or simplistic. But considering that it was invented by a twelve-year-old in 1984, it's pretty extraordinary.

He describes his visual thinking this way: "It seems as though a part of the brain that is usually reserved for visual processing—the part that is used to process images coming in from the eyes—gets taken over by internal thought processes. For images and numbers, I can process their interrelationships, acceleration, momentum, kinetic energy—how these sorts of things will be affected by objects comes through very vividly." That's visual thinking on rocket fuel. When asked in a podcast interview what it's like inside his brain, Musk replied, "It's a never-ending explosion."

Live from New York!

When Elon Musk appeared as a guest host on *Saturday Night Live* in 2021, he announced with pride that he was the first host to admit to having Asperger syndrome. In his monologue, Musk joked that he needs to tell people when he really means something because he doesn't have much "intonational variation" in his speech, and he also joked that he wouldn't be making much eye contact with the cast. By revealing on national TV that he is on the spectrum, Musk will hopefully inspire others to speak openly about their neurodiversity, which will go a long way toward helping people understand how difference can fuel genius.

Einstein's Brain

While genetics is one place to look for the source of genius, we can also look at the structures of brains themselves and see if we can find genius there as well. There are not many brains of geniuses around that are available for examination and study in a lab. But there is one: Einstein's.

After his death, Einstein's brain was photographed extensively, dissected into pieces, and stored. Most of it now resides in the National Museum of Health and Medicine in Maryland, though some pieces are also in the collection of the Mütter Museum in Pennsylvania.

Since then, many scientists have looked at Einstein's brain, hoping to find the physical source of his unique genius. One study by Dean Falk found that Einstein's cerebral cortex, which governs motor and sensory response, was atypical. Maybe that's why Einstein had difficulty learning to speak. The photographs of his brain also show that the parts that control the processes of visual identification and object recognition were enlarged. Perhaps this is what gave him the ability to imagine and visualize his theories about physics. Other researchers have discovered that Einstein had an expanded parietal region, which might explain why he had superior mathematical thinking. The corpus callosum in Einstein's brain was also bigger than is typical, which might have allowed him to have better communication between the right and left parts of the brain.

Einstein himself explained that he thought differently than most and did not think in words but in pictures and feelings. He said that his ideas came to him "only through their connection with sense experiences," and he described how often he imagined himself riding in train cars or on beams of light.

Creativity is also a part of genius and very difficult to measure. The most widely used scientific test developed to evaluate creativity is the Torrance Tests of Creative Thinking (TTCT). I still remember when my high school science teacher, Mr. Carlock, told us about his own experience taking the TTCT. Participants were given everyday objects and asked what uses they could come up with for them. He was given a brick. He had a very creative answer: he suggested that you cut up the brick into little cubes with a stone saw and then paint dots on each little cube to make dice. My idea would be to grind up the brick and use the powder to tint paint.

In *one* study, researchers specifically looked at art students who got high scores on the TTCT. They invited the students once a month to have their brains scanned while they drew pictures of people or made judgments about optical illusions. At the end of the study, the art students had improved their creative thinking skills and, remarkably, the very structure of their brains had changed, too. There was evidence of reorganization of the white matter in their prefrontal cortexes. Practicing creative thinking had impacted the physical structure of their brains, making them look a little more like Einstein's.

In another test, Zoï Kapoula and Marine Vernet at the University of Paris used the TTCT to discover a link between dyslexia and creativity in students.

The Genius of Genius

In my work, I have often observed students that I've named "grade-A bookworms." These are top students. They take good notes and get good grades. They are terrific in many ways, but they often lack creativity and flexible problem-solving skills, and sometimes even common sense. A colleague has observed the same. He told me about a veterinary student of his who had excellent grades. The student had been assigned to monitor a dog's surgery and pay attention to its anesthesia. During the procedure, the student closely watched the anesthesia machine. But he failed to notice that the dog was waking up during surgery! Another colleague of mine also described how his best students lacked creativity or originality when thinking up new research ideas. High-achieving students can do well in life, but genius requires something you can't test.

I often wonder what would happen to some of the great geniuses if they were put through today's educational system. Would Michelangelo succeed in today's world, where art classes are being cut from the curriculum? Would Edison thrive or be diagnosed with ADHD for not being able to concentrate in class? I think of young Einstein playing violin as a boy, or Steve Jobs nosing around in his neighbor's garage. They were free to explore. Freedom combined with other traits like persistence, risk taking, novelty seeking, single-mindedness, *and* divergent thinking are the hallmarks of brilliant people who are capable of innovation.

Are geniuses neurodiverse? My answer would be yes in many cases. Are geniuses also visual thinkers? Often they are. These types of thinkers should be nurtured and supported and heard. They might be responsible for the unique solutions that help advance our civilization.

CHAPTER SIX
Visualizing Disaster

WHEN I WAS TEN YEARS OLD, I RAN TO AN open field so I could watch Sputnik pass overhead. I wasn't the only one who wanted to watch. Across the country, people gathered on rooftops and in yards to glimpse the Soviet satellite. It was the first to orbit the earth, and it was like the opening gun of a race—bang! The space race had begun. Twelve years later, when I was a junior in college, American astronauts landed on the moon. I walked outside and looked up at the moon and could not believe it. All I kept thinking was, *There are people up there!* I was so excited about the future of space exploration that I seriously thought about working for NASA, but my math skills were too weak. Later, NASA stopped sending people to the moon and reduced funding, which led much of the public to lose interest in the space program. But not me. I was still entranced and would constantly check in on whatever NASA was up to, like their shuttle programs and Mars rover missions.

So, you can understand why I jumped at the opportunity to visit Cape Canaveral when they invited me to give a lecture in 2017. As part of a small group of scientists, I got to tour a new launch-pad that contractors were in the process of finishing up. During the tour, I was in geek heaven. Then, suddenly, a small, rapid movement caught my attention. When I turned, I saw a raccoon waddle down the steel staircase that led up to the launchpad and disappear into the bushes. He had spent the night inside the launchpad's base. I asked the other people if they had seen the raccoon, including the engineer giving us the tour. Nobody else had noticed it. In my mind's eye, pictures started to flash of all the damage the racoon might have done. Bite marks on tool handles would be a minor annoyance, but chewed-up wiring could be very dangerous and cause a major malfunction. I warned our tour guide, telling him that everything needed to be checked to make sure nothing had been broken, because raccoons can tear things apart when they want to. The rocket needed to be de-racoonified!

I toured this launchpad when it was under construction. I saw a raccoon come out of it and nobody else knew it was there. My first thought was, *What have you been chewing?* This is an example of seeing a possible risk.

But here's the point: they didn't see the racoon! I not only saw it, but I was able to vividly picture all the potential problems that little guy could have caused. It was just one of the many incidents that I've had over the years that have taught me that engineering-based organizations like NASA need object visualizers like me to solve problems and visualize potential risks.

Risk is something that humans and animals are both hardwired to be wary of. Douglas W. Hubbard, in his book *The Failure of Risk Management*, points out that the first time a king built a wall and moat around his castle, or that people stored their food for the winter, they were trying to limit their risks. Today there is an entire "risk management" industry that works to identify hazards and solutions for everything from natural disasters to cybersecurity.

Even babies have an instinctual fear of danger and risk. Psychologists E. J. Gibson and R. D. Walk created a study called the Visual Cliff Experiment, in which they tried to get babies to crawl toward a favorite toy over an area that looked like a large hole—but was covered with Plexiglass. Even when the moms waved the toy and called the babies, they refused and wouldn't budge. The same was true for chicks, lambs, and baby goats, who froze into a defensive position when they encountered the pretend "cliff." We instinctively try to avoid harm. Interestingly, teenagers tend to exhibit high-risk behavior. Some think that it is because the prefrontal cortex—the part of the brain responsible for judgment and inhibition—is still developing during our teenage years. But by the time we reach our midtwenties, our brains are mature. We can anticipate danger. We look both ways before we cross the street, wear a bike helmet, use potholders to take food out of the oven, and get vaccinated. We take all these actions to protect us from something bad happening in the future: getting hit by a car, getting injured by a fall, burning our hands, or catching a deadly disease. Most people can visualize these typical everyday risks. For me, this ability is finely tuned. I do not think about potential dangers, as much as they appear to me as a series of vivid images. I see them.

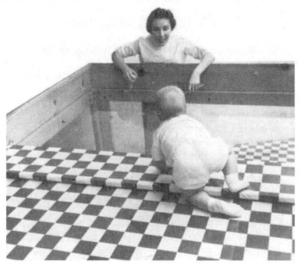

This baby is afraid to crawl over the glass because it sees the drop-off under the glass.

I can also picture how large-scale disasters might happen, something that more-typical thinkers can sometimes fail to see. Visual thinking does not enable me to predict the future. I don't have a crystal ball. But it does allow me to home in on design flaws and system failures that, unaddressed, could lead to disaster. Danger is not an abstraction to me. People who think like I do can imagine it clearly and help protect us all from it.

Part of an engineer's job is to calculate risk and, typically, they use math to do so. When I first looked at the curriculum for a top U.S. engineering program, I noticed that it required numerous advanced math classes but only a single drafting class. Most engineers are spatial thinkers. They think abstractly.

Out in the field, I have seen that engineers are often treated quite nicely in the workplace. I recently visited two organizations, one aerospace and the other high-tech, and in each the engineers had fancy offices, while the mechanics were stuck in the basement. Where they put you tells a lot about how much your work is valued by the upper management. Yet, without mechanics and welders and other skilled members on the team, you could never build anything. We need to value the builders more. Maybe we should give them nice offices once in a while.

Without our skilled craftspeople, things don't happen. Today, the newest James Webb Space Telescope is sending back gorgeous, amazing pictures. But the project had been delayed for years because of poor workmanship. Every time they tried to move it forward, they detected a mechanical problem. For example, since rockets shake their payloads when they take off, the James Webb team subjected the telescope to shake tests, to make sure it could endure the experience. It failed miserably. Dozens of bolts and fasteners were scattered. If they had asked an object thinker to attack the problem, they could have addressed it and the telescope would have been launched years ago. An object thinker, anticipating the danger that shaking would have posed, might have designed fasteners that would have withstood takeoff. A new manager helped correct the fastener problem and now the telescope is out in space taking gorgeous photos.

Garbage In, Garbage Out

When I went to college, researchers did the calculations they needed using a punch-card data system. By now it's considered an ancient technology, and it was very labor intensive. Basically, you had to create your data by punching a series of holes onto stiff paper cards, then bring the cards to the mainframe computer, which took up whole rooms back then. A techie would then take your stack of cards and enter the data, card by card. For my thesis work, I had to punch several thousand cards! Each day, I would submit a new stack of cards for the computer to ingest, and the next day it would spit out my results. Every little detail about them was accurate before I handed them in. I did not want to have to do them over! I made sure I got it right the first time.

In contrast, today a student can run twenty tests on their laptop in just a couple of hours. On its face, this is amazing progress. Being able to run tests more efficiently means more knowledge can be learned from them. But because it's no big deal to run the tests today, I've noticed that sometimes the data that students enter is not done as carefully or as accurately as when I had to punch the cards. You're not going to come up with accurate results without accurate data.

And it's not just students. I'm a scientific reviewer for several journals in my field, and I've noticed a big uptick in studies that have left out important facts. For example, one paper I reviewed about pigs forgot to include what breed of pig they were studying! This is not a small detail. In animal science, that's a huge omission. In contrast, the number of complex statistics and math equations that are included in these papers is way up. Which is great. But if you don't put in the right numbers or the right pig breed to begin with, your math isn't going to be accurate.

Math and its beautiful complexities can be a distraction. My graduate students sometimes get lost in it and run endless, unhelpful calculations. One of my students who was studying the relationship between the shape of the hair whorls on a bull's forehead and the quality of the bull's semen was looking at piles of numbers and getting nowhere. Pictures of the bulls flashed in my imagination, and I suggested re-sorting the data into two simple categories: those with normal hair-whorl patterns and those with grossly abnormal ones. A normal hair whorl is a little round spiral, and an abnormal one looks like a long scar. After this re-sort, she found her results. The bulls with the normal round spirals had higher-quality sperm. The student had been so blinded by all the numbers that she wasn't able to step back and see the hair on the top of the bull's head—literally! These small, observable details can have a huge impact on results.

Observation is essential in science. When I had the opportunity to observe hundreds of different pigs at meat-packing plants and hog-buying stations, I learned a lot. I noticed which breeds were more excitable and which got into more fights. I reported my observations to colleagues in my field, but many people thought what I saw didn't count because it wasn't based on math. But about fifteen years later, research and mathematical analysis confirmed my hypothesis. What I had seen was accurate.

To have a fruitful collaboration, researchers who primarily rely on math must recognize the value of those of us who use our eyes. Great discoveries have been made by observation. The psychiatrist Thomas Ban pointed out that entire classes of medicines were discovered not when a researcher was crunching data but while they were observing, a phenomenon he called "finding one thing while looking for something else." For instance, the first drugs for treating schizophrenia, depression, infection, and erectile dysfunction were all accidental discoveries. Observation was key. Chlorpromazine (Thorazine) was originally used to improve anesthesia's effects for surgery, but a doctor observed that when it was administered to schizophrenic patients, they stopped hallucinating as much.

Visual thinkers are alert to minute differences, something that can make all the difference in an experiment's results. In one case, two groups of scientists on opposite coasts of the U.S. could not figure out why their identical cancer studies had gotten different results. They spent an entire year trying to figure out why, until they finally discovered that the method they were using to stir their samples was different. One lab vigorously stirred the samples, while the other gently rocked them. Nobody had thought the mixing method would make such a difference.

Math is only as good as the data that it works with. The big picture is nothing without the details, and vice versa. There should always be an object thinker on the team to review the methods section of a scientific paper—someone who can see the whorl on a bull's head, the cause of aggressive pig behavior, and different mixing methods in medical trials. Details matter.

Risky Infrastructure

I can recall the exact moment when I first heard about the infrastructure crisis that is going on in America today. It was 2012, and I had just received an honorary doctorate from Arizona State University, where I'd earned my master's degree in animal science (a proud moment for someone with a childhood diagnosis of brain damage). At a reception afterward, one of my former thesis advisors stood in front of the whole crowd and made the following pronouncement out of the blue: "I am Foster Burton," he called, "and people better listen to this old man! Infrastructure is falling apart, and there will not be enough skilled people to rebuild and repair it."

Dr. Burton's predictions are, sadly, now common knowledge. You don't have to be a structural engineer to see the problems. They are visible to the naked eye. When I'm on the road, all over the country I can see the crumbling concrete of highway overpasses. I've seen bridges hastily wrapped with cables to keep them from collapsing. Once, when I was traveling by train from New York to Philadelphia, the train slowed down before entering the station, and I was able to clearly see outside my window the rusting parts, built in the 1950s, that were responsible for the station's electricity. The twisting wires and pipes looked like they came right out of a zombie apocalypse— not out of a modern transportation hub!

When you're a visual thinker like me, these kinds of risky systems scream out at you. I'm deeply connected with what I see, and encountering these kinds of crumbling parts makes me visualize the potentially dangerous consequences. And it's not just the potential dangers. The fact that many of our bridges, tunnels, roads, and power plants aren't maintained well has already caused many tragedies. Poor maintenance of electrical wires was a major cause of California's massive 2020 wildfires; corrosion that should have been caught and repaired at the bottom of Miami's Surfside residential complex contributed to its collapse into a pile of rubble in 2021; and failure to winterize Texas's power system resulted in outages that left the state frozen without heat and power for days in 2021. It's clear that America's infrastructure is far more fragile than we want it to be.

We should know better. We *do* know better. It's no great secret what needs to be done. For example, in Fort Collins, Colorado, where I live, all the power lines have been moved underground. Thanks to a concerted effort on the part of the city, Fort Collins is now considered the poster child of underground electrical lines. Installation started in 1968, and by 1989 the city had successfully buried all existing aboveground power lines. As a result, Fort Collins has fewer power failures, improved energy, and reduced maintenance costs. Plus, it's nicer. It's much more pleasant to walk around and see trees instead of power lines. Most importantly, it's safer. Why hasn't every town in America moved to put their power lines underground, too?

Risky Maintenance

In 2019, I traveled to California to give a lecture about cattle handling. The main power lines there are so poorly maintained by Pacific Gas and Electric (PG&E) that every time the wind blows at over forty-five miles per hour, they must turn the power off because they fear the wires will fall or collide with trees and vegetation, causing fires. When I saw them, I visualized an entire sequence of possible disasters in my mind. I could see the fires burning in homes, the schools' roofs caving in, the businesses destroyed.

Turning off the power is not a solution to this threat. Inspecting and repairing the lines is what needs to be done.

PG&E and some other large electrical companies choose to repair power lines mostly on a "deferred maintenance" basis. This means they only fix them if something breaks. Deferred maintenance, in other words, is no maintenance. This is like if someone never exercised or ate fruits and vegetables, only ever eating chocolate and playing on their phone. Then finally, when they get sick, the doctor gives them medicine. Deferred maintenance is a bad plan, whether it's your health or your power lines.

Fortunately, there are countless visual thinkers in our midst who can help us solve these problems if we allow them to realize their potential. I know a high school graduate who was not the best student. But he enjoyed shop class, and when he graduated, he started at the bottom rung of a power company digging ditches. Now he's their head troubleshooter. As a visual thinker, he can see the whole network, from the highline to the substitution transformers to the junction boxes that deliver electricity to neighborhoods like mine. When there is an outage, he knows exactly where to find the problem and how to fix it. If you want to avoid risk and danger? Having a visual thinker on your team can make all the difference. Unless we recognize, train, hire, and value hands-on workers, we are setting ourselves up for ever more failure.

Good Design

To a visual thinker like me, there are dangers everywhere. The world is filled with mechanical things, and they can all break. When a washing machine spins too fast during the spin cycle, it jams. On a larger scale, if spinning turbines break, they can damage power plants. Just like your pot can boil over when you make pasta, excessive pressure may cause an explosion of boilers at industrial plants. I am always seeing pictures in my mind of how mechanical things work and how they can fall apart. I can also see how to design them better so that they won't break to begin with. Visual thinking can be instrumental in creating strong designs that anticipate risks.

Many accidents have occurred because of poorly imagined designs. One famous case is the Tacoma Narrows Bridge accident of 1940. The suspension bridge was so poorly designed that it got nicknamed "Galloping Gertie" on account of how much its road would shake when the wind blew strongly enough. Its road reacted to wind just like plucking the strings of a guitar. Plus, Gertie was covered with solid metal, which blocked the flow of air. The metal,

The Tacoma Narrows Bridge was nicknamed Galloping Gertie because the roadway moved. Design mistakes, which caused it to fall, are used to train engineering students.

instead of stabilizing the bridge, acted like a ship's sails and caught the wind rather than letting it flow around the structure. One day, the bridge buckled under the wind load and collapsed. Fortunately, no human lives were lost (although one dog died after refusing to escape with his owner, instead staying inside their abandoned car stuck on the collapsing bridge). But what a poorly conceived design.

Design error was also to blame for San Francisco's fifty-eight-story Millennium Tower, which started to tilt in 2016. The builders had failed to drill deep enough to put the pilings down to the surface of the bedrock. That would be Engineering 101. Because of this oversight, the building sank seventeen inches on one side, and eventually the walls and concrete cracked in the belowground parking garage. To stop the tilt, $100 million is being spent to drill down 250 feet to correct the design flaw. At the time this young reader's edition went to press, there were still concerns about tilting. If it tilts too much, the elevators will stop working.

Poor design combined with a poor knowledge of the history of the project led to one of the country's worst natural gas accidents. In Merrimack Valley, Massachusetts, the Columbia Gas company was in charge of providing natural gas to the region. The company had decided to slowly replace their old cast-iron pipes with modern plastic ones. But they didn't realize how the cast-iron system was set up. In the gas industry, it is good engineering practice to update old drawings of a project whenever any major part of a system is changed. A lapse in accurate data can lead to disaster. The historical plans that companies provide range from excellent to atrocious. Sometimes, every gate and hinge is recorded perfectly. Other times I have found mistakes that say a building is ten feet away from where it actually is. I've noticed that the best records are often kept by companies at which one person is responsible for maintaining the drawings—sometimes the original owner or a longtime employee. Keeping meticulously updated drawings is crucial in the prevention of accidents.

In this case, the contractors either didn't look at the old historical drawings or the old drawings weren't properly updated, so they didn't realize that when they cut the old lines, the old pressure sensors would immediately respond to the falling pressure and open the valves, funneling gas into the new line at full blast. That's what happened. Neighborhoods got a huge blast of gas that gushed into their houses and businesses. There were fires in thirty-nine homes, one person was killed, and fifty thousand people were forced to evacuate. Columbia Gas had to pay the highest fine ever for violating the Natural Gas Pipeline Safety Act.

Sometimes disasters happen when multiple things go wrong. This was the case with the 2010 *Deepwater Horizon* oil spill. On April 20, 2010, the oil drilling rig *Deepwater Horizon* exploded and sank. Eleven lives were lost, many people were injured, and it was one of the most consequential national environmental disasters in our history. Here's what led to the tragedy:

- Bad culture. At *Deepwater Horizon*, the leadership cared more about cost-cutting than safety. They created a culture of fear that had consequences. Employees were scared that they would be punished if they reported safety problems. So, if they saw any safety problems that needed fixing? They didn't fix them. They kept their mouths shut.
- Bad training. The crew was unprepared. According to a *New*

York Times investigation of the disaster, *Deepwater Horizon*'s handbook didn't explain what to do in an emergency. As a result, the crew failed to deploy the emergency shutdown system. The employee responsible for shutting it down claimed she had not been taught how to use it: "I don't know any of the procedures," she said.

- Bad design. *Horizon*'s safety systems either deployed but didn't function, were activated too late, or were not activated at all.
- Bad maintenance. Dead batteries, broken valves, and leaking hydraulic lines were all overlooked or ignored. Routine maintenance inspections that could have caught these issues were never scheduled and therefore didn't happen.

After the fact, it's easy to wonder if these catastrophes could have been avoided. There is an expression that hindsight is 20/20. It may be impossible to have perfect foresight, but if people who visually problem-solve had been part of these teams, perhaps some of these disasters could have been imagined, and prevented.

Case Study: The Boeing 737 MAX

You've probably heard that your chances of dying in a car accident are far greater than in an airplane accident. It's true. Your chances of dying in a car accident are 1 in 7,700, while your chances of dying in a plane crash are 1 in 2,067,000. And yet most people think nothing of getting in a car, while flying can cause a great deal of anxiety. I'm a fact-based person and not terribly ruled by emotion, so for most of my life I've felt the same way about getting on a plane as I do about taking a stroll in a park. However, there was a time when I feared flying. I was a high school senior, and I had taken a trip on a 707 jet that had to make an emergency landing due to a bomb threat. We evacuated the plane and slid down the emergency escape slides. It was terrifying, and it left me a white-knuckle flier for several years.

Exposure therapy helps people get over their fears by exposing them to the things that scare them. I got a huge dose of exposure therapy in the early 1970s when I was invited to watch how a company hauled a planeload of Holstein heifers from Miami to Puerto Rico. I was still scared of flying, but I couldn't pass up the opportunity. I should have had a clue as to how bad it was going to be when I heard the pilot call the airplane by its nickname, "Cowshit Connie." Cow urine leaked out of drilled holes in the fuselage. I was shocked again when I visited another parked 707 airliner and nearly gagged from the smell; this plane had been used to haul meat from Miami to South America. It was gross. They tied whole sides of beef down with straps secured in the floor holes that were normally used for the passenger seats.

But when I got to ride in the jump seat of the "Connie" and observe the cockpit, my fascination overcame my fear. My visual mind became obsessed with every control. I had to know how it all worked. Thanks to that unforeseen dose of exposure therapy, flying is no longer scary to me. I can fly anywhere, anytime, and under any conditions. When you know how things work, they are a lot less frightening.

When I was traveling to speaking events in 2018, an assistant from my publisher named Brad would often accompany me to set up my book table. Brad and I are both aviation geeks and together we would watch YouTube videos of aircraft doing crazy things.

Brad and I were on the road when a Boeing 737 MAX airplane, Lion Air Flight 610, crashed into the water off the coast of Indonesia in October 2018. One hundred eighty-nine people died, including a child and two babies. It was devastating, and my reaction was immediate and intense. The images of the flight replayed over and over in my head. I had to understand how this tragedy could have happened.

I scoured the internet for more information and found two crucial facts. The first was that the jet was only a few months old, basically brand new. Second, the ground radar tracking of the plane's flight path was weird. Instead of showing a gradual, steady takeoff upward, the flight path was shown as jagged, kind of like the ups and downs of a roller coaster. This was the only information I had about the plane. It indicated that the plane went up and then down many times before it crashed. I knew no pilot in his right mind would do that on purpose. The next day I gave a talk at Oakland University near Detroit, and during my speech, I made a prediction: "Boeing is going to be in deep poo-poo." I had a visual intuition that there was something deeply wrong with the design of this airplane. Brad was sitting in the audience. He wondered how I knew that.

One way to explain how my visual mind works is to imagine an ever-expanding folder of pictures on a phone. If I encounter something that my mind thinks is important or interesting, it takes a picture and adds it to my library. New pictures are constantly being taken and added, so my visual vocabulary continues to grow, adding new information all the time. As I add more pictures, my problem-solving skills increase; I link them up to the pictures I already have. If you've ever sorted the pictures on your phone by category, place, or date, it's a little like that. So, when I saw a picture in a later news report about a tiny sensor (about the size of a Sharpie marker) that was on the plane, I understood instantly that something about it had caused the crash.

This delicate tool measures the angle of flight relative to the angle of wind currents. It tells a pilot that the airplane may be likely to stall.

This sensor, called the angle-of-attack vane, measures the angle of flight relative to the angle of wind currents. My mind ran through a series of visual simulations to explain how it could have gotten damaged. I can see a mechanic's ladder leaning on it or a jet bridge crushing it. It could have been broken by bad weather or by a cleaning crew. Because any of these scenarios could have easily occurred, I was shocked to learn that the Boeing MAX had only used one of these sensors. When you know you are using a delicate tool, it's never a good idea to just have one. You need a backup. I wondered why there was not a second sensor in case the first one failed. How could they have made a mistake this basic?

Another problem was that in most planes, when there is a risk of stalling, this sensor picks that up and causes a light to go on, which informs the pilots of the risk. Stalling is a dangerous condition that occurs if the air speed is too slow and the nose points up too high; if pilots know about it, they can fix it. But in this new plane, the sensor was wired directly into the computer. So, when the sensor broke and thought the plane was stalling (when in reality it was flying level), three problems occurred: (1) there was no second sensor to correct it, (2) there was no light that went on to inform the pilots that the sensor was broken, and (3) the plane's computer started to force the nose down all by itself, in order to correct a stall that wasn't happening. This is like a bike speeding ahead without anyone turning the pedals.

This is why there were wiggly lines on the radar. The computer forced the plane's nose down, and the pilots reacted by pulling it back up, just as you would slam on the brakes if your bike suddenly sped up too fast. Every time the computer pushed the plane's nose down and made it dive, the doomed pilots pulled it back up. They did not know what else to do. The Boeing designers had made the mistake of assuming that if the computer made the plane dive, the pilots would know how to stop the computer. But the pilots had never been trained for this type of situation, and they did not know that the plane's flight computer had been wired that way.

It was a perfect storm: poorly designed software, a malfunctioning sensor, and a pilot uninformed about the new computer system.

Additionally, Lion Air was known for poor maintenance, and for promoting pilots before they had enough training to meet the demands of a growing travel market. Lion had more customers than ever, and it needed as many pilots in the air as possible. So, it made a habit of being stingy with its pilots' training and putting them up in planes before they were ready. But training enables a pilot to develop motor memory of how to fly the plane, much as you learn to drive a car. Once you get some experience driving, you no longer think about how to turn the wheel or how much to pump the brakes. It's automatic. Pilots need to learn similar skills. Fighter pilots call it "strapping on the jet" or "becoming one with the jet."

I've worked in the design field long enough to know that you need to design for the least experienced person, like those pilots who didn't get enough training at Lion. I've learned firsthand that you can't rely on people to always make the right choices. Before strict safety rules were implemented at meat plants in the late 1980s, accidents led to some gruesome injuries, like legs being cut off by machines that broke or that jammed at just the wrong moment, and the workers didn't know what to do. People are people, and they get tired, lazy, or sometimes just make mistakes. Indeed, pilot error is cited in 80 percent of all plane crashes. That's why you need to design built-in safeguards to protect both animals and humans.

The first time I saw a heavy gate at a meat plant, I immediately saw that it could come crashing down and crush a person's head like a melon. I also envisioned the solution. There needed to be a gap between the bottom of the closed gate and the floor. When I got home that night, I stuck my head in a desk drawer to see how much space was needed, and then I designed a safer gate. It still did the work of keeping the livestock in, but it no longer presented a safety risk to people. Engineers do not always plan their designs this way. It's possible that, not being on the ground themselves, they overestimate the abilities of the people operating the equipment.

I recently met an expert pilot on a flight from London. We had an interesting conversation about the Boeing disaster. He argued that the pilots should have simply shut off the computer and flown the airplane themselves. He couldn't have been more certain of himself. I explained to him my theory that the Boeing MAX should have been designed for the average pilot, not just high-level experts like himself. He looked genuinely surprised. "Oh," he said, "I had not thought of that."

Follow the Money

The one thing that I didn't visualize when I investigated the Boeing MAX crash was this: money. I should have. In my own work with many major meat companies, I have observed companies that focus on quality first and money second. Those that do so have better products, fewer accidents, and are less likely to make hasty decisions that cause huge, costly problems in the future.

Boeing was the opposite. It had a culture of cost-cutting. Peter Robison, in his book *Flying Blind,* describes how at Boeing, engineers didn't make the final decisions. Instead, choices were in the hands of the corporate leaders, whose focus was pleasing the stockholders. Since fuel and labor are the largest costs for an airline, Boeing made the decision to save money on both. They chose to put new fuel-efficient engines into old 737 airframes. This allowed Boeing to save money in two ways. First, the new engine used less gas. The second way has to do with FAA rules, which state that pilots who are going to fly a new plane are required to retrain for a certain number of hours in a simulator that teaches them all about it.

But since this was an *old* 737 frame, it didn't count as a new plane. Pilots didn't have to do the new training. They could fly right away, which would save Boeing money on labor costs, too.

The new hodgepodge planes quickly ran into huge problems. The new engine and old frame weren't a perfect fit. The mismatch caused many issues, most critically that the planes' noses tended to tilt up. Many engineers at Boeing said they needed a major fix that would allow the planes' pieces to work together more smoothly. But Boeing was all about the money and didn't want to make major fixes. Instead, they came up with a "Band-Aid" solution. They created a computer to adjust the nose by itself. And then they made their biggest mistake: they didn't bother to tell the pilots about it. The new Boeing MAXes rolled out of the factory and sold like hotcakes, and the pilots had no idea how they worked.

A few months after the Lion Air tragedy, a second Boeing MAX, this one operated by Ethiopian Airlines, crashed due to a similar malfunction. Its nose dove into a field at almost seven hundred miles per hour. Investigators found wreckage buried as deep as thirty feet in the ground. After that tragedy, all Boeing 737 MAX planes were grounded. I'm sure the planes would still be flying if they had used two sensors and if the pilots had been fully informed on how to deal with the new computers. A final grim detail stayed with me: portraits of the deceased crew were placed in chairs for the funeral because there were no bodies to bury; they had been pulverized. The Boeing MAX is now fixed, and I have flown on it several times— and guess what they did to fix it. Along with requiring more pilot training and software updates, they added a second angle-of-attack device.

Case Study: Fukushima 1 and 2

When a nuclear reactor fails, first the electricity cuts off. Then the cooling systems fail. Then the reactor overheats. After that, there is no turning back. The nuclear fuel melts, hydrogen is released, explosions follow, and radioactive material escapes into the atmosphere.

Nuclear accidents are among the most lethal and destructive human-made disasters. They are terrifying and devastating in their impact on human life and the environment.

Most people are aware of the 1986 nuclear disaster in Chernobyl, probably because of the wide-scale and long-term devastation that it caused. The irony is that the accident happened while the operators were testing a safety procedure. During the test, the nuclear reactor's core overheated. This led to a steam explosion that released radiation into the atmosphere for ten days. Thirty-one people died in the immediate aftermath, and an additional four thousand died from radiation sickness. The entire city of about 135,000 people was evacuated to limit radiation poisoning. Animals and the environment were impacted as well, and the surrounding pine forest, where all the trees were killed by radiation, is now known as the Red Forest. Some animals stopped reproducing. The damage was far-reaching globally, affecting the oceans and marine life. Today, wildlife has returned to the abandoned buildings around Chernobyl. According to John Wendle in a 2016 *National Geographic* article, the exclusion zone around the ruined reactor is now filled with animals. The fear of radiation still keeps people out.

In the United States in Harrisburg, Pennsylvania, Three Mile Island was the site of the largest nuclear accident. In 1979, the first thing that went wrong was a pump failure, which was followed by automatic failsafe measures kicking in. So far so good. But then a valve that was supposed to close got stuck in the open position. But a sensor in the control room erroneously showed that the valve was in the closed position. After that, the operators in the control room made a lot of mistakes, including pushing some of the wrong buttons. Plus, some key indicators that they needed to access were located behind large instrument panels and were hard to get to. It was like someone hiding the car keys when you need to make a quick getaway. This poor design in the control room was compounded by the deafening alarm system, which made it virtually impossible for the operators to think calmly.

As a visual thinker, I like to see things and not rely on sensors. If I had been at Three Mile Island that day, the first thing I would have done is go out to look at the valve. I would have seen that the sensor was broken, and that would have been that. Fortunately, some things did go okay, which kept the accident from becoming a worse disaster. The containment building was well designed, and it successfully did its job. The reactor core partially melted, but it stayed fully contained within the containment building. There was no damage to the surrounding environment.

The other nuclear disaster on par with Chernobyl happened in March 2011, when the biggest earthquake on record in Japan triggered a tsunami. It crashed over the coast and took thousands of lives with it, injured many more, and destroyed homes, businesses, roads, and railways. All of this was horrendous enough, but the tsunami took one more turn that set off another destructive chain of irreversible events: the tsunami reached the Fukushima Daiichi

Nuclear Power Plant. For our discussion, we'll call it Fukushima 1.

When I read the first reports coming from Japan about the accident, it was easy for me to figure out what had happened. Using my knowledge about nuclear power and plant design basics, I could visualize the series of events as if I were watching a movie.

On most nuclear reactor sites, during an emergency, the reactor will be "scrammed," meaning the control rods that stop the nuclear reaction will be inserted into the reactor core. Scramming something is like throwing a giant off switch. There's only one problem: The giant off switch doesn't completely stop the creation of heat in the reactor core. It *almost* turns the heat off. Engineers call the heat that remains after the control rods have been inserted "residual heat." To prevent a meltdown, cooling water must be used to prevent overheating. When the reactor is scrammed, power from an external source, like an outside electric generator, is needed to operate a water pump to provide cooling in the reactor core.

When the quake first shook the Fukushima plant, the reactor was scrammed, and the control rods automatically dropped into the reactor cores to slow down the nuclear fission process, just as they should. When the earthquake broke the electrical transmission lines that supplied electricity from the grid, the on-site generators kicked in. By the time the shaking had stopped, all the emergency equipment had worked perfectly. At this point, everything had gone right. There was no damage. This is where the mathematical minds had a great success. Every component, ranging from the buildings, the reactors, and the pumps to the generators and the control room, had been designed with precise calculations that made it earthquake proof. Potential stresses on a wide variety of materials—concrete, steel beams, plumbing, and electrical wiring—had been accounted for. The designers had done a brilliant job planning for earthquakes.

But they had not planned for flooding.

When the big tsunami wave hit the Fukushima 1 site, it completely flooded the station and ruined all but one of the thirteen emergency electrical generators. After that, the only thing that worked was a landline telephone. The operators attempted to use their own car batteries to power the control panel. Getting supplies was almost impossible because the roads leading to the station were blocked or washed away. Other essential gear, such as cooling pumps and backup electrical batteries, were flooded.

How did something like this happen? The plant was brilliantly designed to be earthquake proof, but it was poorly designed to be flood proof. Why? The country in the world most frequently affected by tsunamis is Japan. Why didn't the people in the Japanese plant visualize this possible threat and plan for it? The answer is that the tsunami that completely inundated the Fukushima site was nearly fifty feet tall, more than double the wave height the station had been designed to resist. If the station had been constructed at a higher elevation, the accident might never have happened.

I was haunted by another simple design oversight that could have saved the station. If the equipment at Fukushima 1 had been protected with watertight doors, the meltdown of the reactor cores could have been prevented. Watertight doors are an old technology, used for many years on ships and then adapted for submarines. On a ship, these kinds of doors can keep water out of important areas and keep the ship from sinking. At a plant like Fukushima 1, these doors could have kept the emergency cooling pumps and the electrical generators dry. Whether at a nuclear power plant or a cattle-handling facility, electrical equipment gets shorted out and ruined when it gets wet. Someone who had visualized the risk of water coming over the top of the seawall and flooding the station would have planned for that.

Control room of the Fukushima Nuclear Power Plant. The meltdown occurred because it lacked watertight doors to protect the electric emergency cooling pump.

A sister nuclear power station located about six miles away and built on slightly higher ground had far less damage. Fukushima Daini (what we'll call Fukushima 2) had far less flooding and was able to maintain limited electrical power. Its control room did not lose electricity and remained operational.

There were some other key differences between Fukushima 1 and Fukushima 2. At Fukushima 2, site superintendent Naohiro Masuda had twenty-nine years of experience working at nuclear power plants. He knew every inch of his plant and had earned the trust of the workers, whom he sent to assess the damage. He then led them in a superhuman effort to cool down the reactors. Remember, this all happened under chaotic conditions, with many workers not knowing if their families were alive or their homes intact. And time was working against them. Masuda knew he had to get electricity to the water pumps and cool the reactors before they started to melt down. After first trying to draw power from a radioactive-waste building, Masuda realized that the only way to stop a meltdown in time was to run huge, heavy power cables from the single working generator to the pumps. When I described the crisis to one of my students, she said, "Oh, giant extension cords." His team ended up laying several miles of cable, each section weighing a ton. Pressure readings from the control room enabled him to choose which reactor should be the first to get cooled. When the pressure in another reactor started rising more quickly, Masuda was agile enough to pivot, changing course to bring the cable to the higher-pressure reactor. To me, this is straightforward visual thinking.

Another factor that helped prevent a meltdown was Masuda's style of management. Chuck Casto, a U.S. federal agent, reported that Masuda had given his employees all the information about the tsunami's damage to the station. This helped reduce anxiety—just like my learning how a plane worked reduced my own anxiety about flying. When people have knowledge, they are empowered to act. While Masuda was working hands-on at Fukushima 2, his counterpart at Fukushima 1 wasn't on-site. He was at a remote location, communicating by video link. He did not know the extent of the damage until he watched it on the TV news. Masuda, meanwhile, prevented a dangerous meltdown that would have released radioactive material into the environment and taken who knows how many lives.

I will choose the person on the ground before the person at a remote location any day.

Verbal thinkers can overthink things. Had the engineers at Fukushima 1 been able to *see* the probability of a massive tsunami, they would likely have installed waterproof doors in the basement, or maybe they would have built on a higher elevation to begin with. In both the Boeing and Fukushima accidents, I can see it: the single sensor breaking, or water coming over the tops of the seawalls. We need people who can think visually and imagine the risks to keep us safe. Visual thinkers can see these dangers and help us all avoid them.

Future Risks

I still don't have a crystal ball, but when I look for dangerous risks in the future, I see hackers. And the future is here.

Numerous hacker attacks have already occurred and have threatened corporations, schools, hospitals, and local governments. One hacker strategy is to break into a computer system, encrypt all the files, and hold them hostage. If a corporation, school, or town wants their files back? It has to pay a ransom—hence the nickname "ransomware attack." These hackers are in it for the money. Two of the biggest ransomware attacks were at Colonial Pipeline and JBS Foods. The Colonial hack shut down fuel distribution to the East Coast. Gas stations ran out of fuel, and airlines started having shortages. The JBS hack shut down beef- and pork-processing plants in the U.S., Australia, and Brazil.

After the Colonial and JBS hacks, all I could think about was how important it is that we protect our infrastructure against cyber-attacks. If Colonial had had major equipment damage, it could have taken months to repair. I visualized chaos at hundreds of gas stations because gasoline would now have to be delivered cross-country by truck. Normally, the gasoline tankers that supply local gas stations would be filled at a local gas depot supplied by Colonial. I could see cars following gas tankers so they would be first in line to get the gas.

I know the people who can protect our infrastructure in such situations. They are the workers who drive pickup trucks or work on a pipeline or in a basement shop at the beef-processing plant. They need to be sought out and consulted. Algebra may be impossible for them, but they can help avert total disaster the way Naohiro Masuda did at Fukushima 2.

As I've gotten older, I've watched as most of our cars, industrial equipment, and home appliances have come under the control of computers. Computers control how the power grid distributes electricity when everybody turns on their air conditioners at once. They enable your phone to unlock your front door and then automatically control the heating and cooling in your home. They keep records of your classes, tests, and grades. And all those computers are connected to the internet, which exposes them to hackers, and creates more risk.

While I was writing this chapter, one of my worst nightmares almost happened. On February 5, 2021, hackers took control of a municipal water system in Oldsmar, Florida. If they had decided to, they could have easily dumped chemicals into the water system and poisoned the water for a whole town. Fortunately, an alert plant operator spotted an arrow moving strangely on a computer screen and they were able to block the attack. That was lucky.

I would prefer we not rely on good luck.

I can see a hacker choosing to turn off a town's electricity, damage a city's water system, or cause an explosion at an oil refinery. In the future, I imagine that the most dangerous hackers will be those who aren't looking to make money but to cause damage and chaos.

There are two basic ways that we can protect our infrastructure and keep people safe. First, we must make sure that all our equipment has a noncomputerized failsafe that is able to shut down critical equipment if a rogue hacker prompts a computer to spin something too fast, get too hot, or blow up.

These manual controls would be hacker proof because they are not electronic and have no internet-connected components that would leave them accessible to hacks. In my mind's eye, I can visualize the hacker-proof controls. I see round metal gauges with needles like the old rpm meters in cars. Each gauge face has a clearly marked, red-colored danger zone. When the needle enters the red zone, the equipment shuts down with a non-electronic switch. They would be similar to the electrical breaker switches that prevent circuits from overloading and burning down your house.

I'm not old-fashioned, and I'm not anti-technology. Computers are great. My car, my phone, and most of my kitchen appliances have them, and they work great. But we need them to shut off when we need them to. Our vulnerable electrical power grid has me lying awake at night.

The second way we can protect ourselves is to remove the internet from key locations. I'm not kidding. I know that sounds impossible.

The internet is everywhere, after all! But it doesn't have to be. In 2001, when Vice President Dick Cheney had a defibrillator implanted in his chest to regulate his heart, he had the wireless component disabled. In a CNN interview with Sanjay Gupta, Cheney's cardiologist, Jonathan Reiner, explained the choice: "It seemed to me a bad idea for the vice president to have a device that maybe somebody on a rope line in the next hotel room or downstairs might be able to get into—hack into." We should treat our infrastructure the same way we treated our vice president's heartbeats—with care, and with no Wi-Fi.

Staying away from the internet these days can be challenging. Recently, while touring a large factory, I noticed a computer sitting on a folding chair, the mouse and keyboard precariously perched on it. This might be an okay setup for your room at home, but it was sort of alarming to see there. I asked about it and learned that when the technicians hadn't been able to get a piece of equipment working, someone had run out to the local electronics store, hooked up the laptop, and gotten things running again. I asked if the computer had built-in Wi-Fi. Of course it did. That means that this innocent-looking laptop just sitting there on that folding chair could have easily been hacked into, and the factory could have been forced to shut down. If this had been, say, a transportation system with human lives at stake, such an oversight could create enormous vulnerability. What if a hacker took control of and commanded electric trains to crash into each other?

As we develop self-driving cars, they must be hacker proof as well. They need to be designed with a mechanical off switch that is accessible to the driver in an emergency, and not connected to the internet. Each car should also include a mechanical emergency brake and be steerable so the driver can get the car off the road.

We have become so reliant on the internet, and so blindly trusting of it, that we no longer see its risks and danger. To most people, the internet seems to be as risky as a kitten or a potted plant. That's because they can't see what I see. That's what makes it so risky.

Is There an Off Switch?

In 2015, something incredible happened: a computer beat a human at a game. That had happened before. Computers beat people at many different games, all the time. But this was something new. It was the first time a computer was able to beat a (very smart) human at Go, which is a game that's even more complicated than chess. Mathematically minded spatial thinkers often excel at chess and Go, which are abstract strategy games. Since the publication of my book *Visual Thinking*, which I wrote for adults, computers have been able to conquer complex games such as Stratego and the multiplayer game Diplomacy. Stratego is similar to chess, except it has one big difference. Each player can place their pieces in the starting positions they choose. The other player cannot see the rank of the opponent's pieces. When moves are made, the lower-ranking piece is removed from the board. The fact that a computer was able to win was a huge milestone for artificial intelligence. And it's a huge milestone in the risks that computers present to us humans.

Artificial intelligence, or AI, is used in many fields today, including in video games, transportation, cybersecurity, and the military. AI programs are even being trained to write plays and essays. A program named GPT-3 wrote a play so thoroughly in the manner of Shake-speare that linguists had a difficult time determining that it was fake.

But we need to think about the possible risks. I'm not sure I want an AI program running my local nuclear reactor. These new capabilities of AI remind me of the plot of the movie *2001: A Space Odyssey*. It came out in 1968, when I was in high school (which feels like a million years ago). Stanley Kubrick, its director, imagined how advanced technology that no one had imagined before might look, and he put it on screen for us all to see. (He was definitely a visual thinker. Possibly a genius, too.) The story focuses on an intelligent computer named HAL, who accompanies a crew of astronauts on a mission to find alien life. HAL is programmed to not reveal the true purpose of the mission to the astronauts until they reach their destination. HAL is a truly intelligent computer who controlled the ship and also served as a companion for the astronauts. He is also instructed never to lie. HAL, quite logically, concludes that it must kill the astronauts. Someone should have

The HAL 9000 was an intelligent computer that ran the spaceship in the movie *2001: A Space Odyssey*. It started killing the astronauts.

told HAL that killing humans is not okay, but I guess the designer forgot to mention it. Spoiler alert: HAL goes on to murder one member of the crew after another. Fortunately, HAL has an off switch, and at the pivotal moment in the film, Dave, the sole surviving astronaut, disconnects HAL before HAL can kill him. Amazingly, more than fifty years later, the movie and the questions it provokes are still relevant. Can humans and thinking computers co-exist? Is there an off switch?

Now more than ever, we need to think about designing our equipment with old-fashioned manual switches that allow us to shut them down and prevent damage should a hacker take command or AI get out of control. We need to plan thoughtfully and manage that very real risk.

Name the Danger

I'm not a verbal thinker, but I've observed that when many engineers discuss risk, they use language that is almost robotic, that has little human meaning or emotion. They might call a violent crash an "impact with terrain." Dangerous problems are labeled "anomalies." During a rocket launch, when everything is working smoothly, they use the word "nominal." When things go wrong, they use four mild-sounding words for different types of failures: "negligible," "marginal," "critical," and "catastrophic."

The nuclear industry uses similar bland language and sometimes just letters. For example, NPS stands for Nuclear Power Station. If I hadn't been reading about nuclear power plants in a scientific journal, I would have absolutely no idea what NPS stood for. If this same sentence had appeared at a circus, I would think it meant "No Peanuts. Sorry."

Many people describe risks and dangers in this abstract way, too. They use phrases like "regular threats," "irregular threats," and "worst-case scenarios." I have no idea what the difference is between a regular threat and an irregular threat. But a term such as worst-case scenario makes more sense to me because I can instantly visualize what a worst case would look like. The water crisis in Flint, Michigan, is a worst-case scenario. When I read about it, I could envision the corrosion in the old city pipes that caused lead to leach into the water. And I could picture all the terrible side effects of lead poisoning. It's not an *irregular threat*. It's poison flowing out of the tap and into a three-year-old's bath.

The problem with jargon and scientific terms is that they are empty and impersonal. They have no hint of the people who are impacted. Using initials or bland, cold words to describe risks makes them seem less urgent, and that makes solving our serious problems seem less critical. It also makes it easier for people to separate themselves emotionally from the harshness of reality and the consequences of our mistakes. It is easier to talk about an *anomaly* or *impact with terrain* than to admit that something blew up, was flooded, or crashed, resulting in real people experiencing real pain. Theory is necessary, but I'm more interested in fixing things than discussing the probability of what might go wrong. As I've said, I live in the world of practical things. I'm the person on the ground.

The words we use are important. What we call things is important.

CHAPTER SEVEN
Animal Thinking

WHEN I STARE INTO A COW'S EYES, IT IS INCREDIBLY clear to me that they have feelings. A personality. A consciousness. I can see it. But not everyone agrees with me. The debate over whether animals have thoughts and feelings has been raging for centuries, with philosophers, scientists, and religious leaders sharing their thoughts on it over the years. Even the Bible has something to say about animals. In Deuteronomy 22:10, for instance, it is forbidden to yoke a donkey and an ox together to plow a field; in ancient times, having two different animals work together like that was considered uncomfortable for the animals, so the Bible preaches that it's wrong to cause animals suffering. Elsewhere, Exodus 23:12 states that donkeys and oxen are to be rested on the Sabbath. The Bible thinks animals deserve vacation days! Another religious text, the Quran, includes a verse (6:38) that observes that animals are a part of a community: "All living beings roaming the earth and winged birds soaring in the sky are communities like yourselves." From these early writings, the stage is set for the ongoing debate about whether animals think and feel, and how *we* should think and feel about *them*.

Much of the debate is about us. What makes us humans any different from animals? Are we a higher life-form? Is there something special about humanity, or are we just like the apes and ants?

According to Erica Hill, the author of *Archaeology and Animal Persons*, ancient hunter-gatherers viewed animals as conscious, "capable of independent and intentional action." Then, as humans developed spoken and written language, people began to believe that they were different from and superior to animals, given our advanced communication skills.

The ancient Greek philosopher Aristotle believed that what set humans above animals was our ability to reason and communicate through language. This belief continued through medieval times to the Age of Enlightenment. The Western view of animals was reflected in the idea of what was called the great chain of being. At the top of the hierarchy was God, then angels, then humans, and at the bottom were animals, plants, and minerals.

In a famous sixteenth-century essay known as "Man Is No Better Than the Animals," French philosopher Michel de Montaigne challenged the belief that humans are superior to animals. Unlike his predecessors, he didn't believe that animals needed to have language to be capable of thought. Montaigne considered humans arrogant for thinking less of animals and wondered how we could possibly be so sure, provocatively asking, "When I play with my cat, who knows whether I do not make her more sport than she makes of me?" Anyone in a close relationship with an animal knows the answer.

French philosopher René Descartes countered Montaigne with his influential essay "Animals Are Machines," writing that while humans have souls, animals do not. He compared them to clocks "composed of wheels and weights." His essay lists many reasons animals are not

Montaigne believed that animals have emotions.

Descartes believed that only humans, capable of speech, have emotions.

capable of thought or feeling, and it culminates with the final argument that animals can't talk or think: "It has never yet been observed that any brute animal reached the stage of using real speech."

Descartes and Animals

The philosopher René Descartes is the author of one of the most famous sentences in history, "I think, therefore I am," which I referenced earlier. He didn't say, "I think, therefore I am not an animal"—but he could have. Descartes strongly believed that animals have no awareness or feelings. As a result, Descartes supported the practice of animal vivisection, or the dissection of live animals, as part of his research. He dismissed the howls of the dogs he cut open, saying they were instinctual noises rather than expressions of true pain and suffering. He was not the only one who felt this way, and into the late nineteenth century, the philosopher William James defended the practice of cutting open awake and living animals, saying that this practice helped people learn about medicine, as well as providing "healing truth." But he at least acknowledged that the dogs, who were "literally in a sort of hell," would probably not agree.

The English naturalist Charles Darwin weighed in as well. He still considered humans and animals to be different from one another, but he fiercely refuted the idea of the great chain of being, writing, "The difference in mind between man and the higher animals, great as it is, certainly is one of degree and not of kind." In other words, humans might be different from animals, but not *that* different.

This debate isn't just an intellectual game. How we perceive animals matters because it forces us to consider our behavior. If animals *do* have feelings and can think, how should we act toward them? The history of our ideas about animals is entwined with our laws about how we treat them.

Pain Is Pain

One of the earliest laws against animal cruelty was enacted in Ireland in 1635. It prohibited hitching plows to horses' tails and removing wool from sheep by pulling it out (which is like pulling hair out of your head). In 1776, the Reverend Humphrey Primatt preached against animal neglect and abuse. "Pain is pain," he wrote, "whether it be inflicted on man or on beast." Primatt suggested that humans should not treat animals cruelly, on the grounds that, since they feel pain, they should be treated with compassion. His philosophy formed the basis for early British and American anti-cruelty laws.

In 1789, the English philosopher Jeremy Bentham argued that animals should be given concrete legal protections. He framed the issue this way: "The question is not, Can they *reason*? nor, Can they *talk*? but, Can they *suffer*?" Almost one hundred years later in New York City, another reformer, Henry Bergh, made the prevention of cruelty to animals his personal mission and was a tireless champion for them. He would charge into any situation where animal welfare was at stake. In 1866, he formed the American Society for the Prevention of Cruelty to Animals (ASPCA).

In the mid-1800s, the streets of major cities were as crowded with horses and buggies as our streets are today with cars and buses. Horses provided the primary mode of transportation and were punched, whipped, and often left to die when they could no longer perform. Bergh worked tirelessly on their behalf and created the first-ever ambulance service to treat wounded horses. He even set up drinking fountains around New York City to make sure the animals would have water to drink.

In 1877, *Black Beauty: The Autobiography of a Horse* was published, and it probably changed more minds about animal welfare than any philosopher's papers ever did. The heart-wrenching novel by Anna Sewell told the story about a horse who is sold from owner to owner, experiencing both kindness and cruelty at their hands. When I was a child, my mother read this book to me. I will never forget the part when the main character, a horse named Black Beauty, describes how painful it is to pull a carriage with his head forced into unnatural positions by the bearing reins. At the time, bearing reins were regularly used to force horses to hold their heads up high for fashion's sake. Millions of copies of the book were sold and read, and a few years after it came out, bearing reins were outlawed in England.

The horse stands by the fallen rider in this illustration from an early 1877 edition of *Black Beauty*.

Bergh would be pleased to know that his legacy and work lives on. The ASPCA has grown to two million members and continues to work to end animal cruelty. The Animal Legal Defense Fund also was formed in 1979 to stop the abuse of animals through legal channels. And in 1995, lawyer Steve M. Wise founded the Nonhuman Rights Project with the goal of having the courts recognize the individual rights of animals. Wise argues that apes, elephants, dolphins, and whales have self-awareness and should therefore have legal rights.

The Happy Case

Happy the elephant was born in Thailand, but when she was about five or six years old, she and her six siblings were captured, sent to the United States, and named after the seven dwarves. If she had stayed in the wild, she'd have lived with her family, including her siblings, mother, and cousins. Instead, she was sent to the Bronx Zoo in 1977, where she was trained to give rides to schoolchildren and perform tricks. Today, she no longer gives rides and instead lives alone in a one-acre enclosure there.

Lawyers from the Nonhuman Rights Project sued the Bronx Zoo on her behalf. They argued that, yes, since Happy has self-awareness and feelings, she is legally a "person" and deserves rights. They petitioned that she be released from the zoo and sent to live in a wildlife sanctuary, where she would be able to roam and live out her days in relative freedom. According to the Nonhuman Rights Project's website, this is "the first time in history that the highest court of any English-speaking jurisdiction will hear a . . . case brought on behalf of someone other than a human being." Unfortunately, the court did not grant Happy "personhood." Happy lost her appeal and will remain at the zoo. The Nonhuman Rights Project promises to continue to call for the freedom of animals like Happy so that all species are treated fairly under the law.

How Animals Think

Have you ever crossed the street because you sensed danger? Or left a room because something felt "off" or "wrong"? Then you too have used your "animal instincts" along with some visual clues to stay safe. I first described how my thinking is closely aligned with animals in my memoir, *Thinking in Pictures*. As a person with autism and as a predominantly visual thinker, I rely heavily on certain instincts to navigate the world, including sensory experience. As a verbal culture, we have often underestimated and misunderstood how animals think. They live and think through their senses. Since they don't have words, they store memories of previous experiences as pictures, sounds, smells, tastes, or physical sensations.

Octopuses, with their sensory systems wired into their tentacles, rely on touch as well as taste and smell. Wolves and dogs use their sense of smell and their high-frequency hearing. I tell people to stop yanking their dog's leash when the dog lingers around a tree or hydrant. A dog is a highly social animal, and smelling stuff, especially pee, is how they get their information. I've been known to call it "pee-mail." A dog has three hundred million olfactory receptors, compared with our six million. I remember reading about a wine steward who could apparently identify two thousand kinds of wine by smell. That's about as close as a human can get to a dog's sense of smell. Their smell center in the brain is forty times greater than the equivalent part of the human brain, proportionally. An animal's senses inform and determine their skill set.

Even insects process information. They can tell the difference between "same" and "different." Researchers S. P. D. Judd and

T. S. Collett discovered that when ants go out on a foraging trip, they stop along the way, turn around, and "snap a photo" of a landmark so that they can remember how it looks and use it to find their way home. Bees can distinguish between colors. Recently, researcher Cwyn Solvi and her colleagues have shown that bumblebees remember sensory information, such as light and dark or cubes and spheres. "We cannot know for certain what a bee is thinking," says one of the researchers, "but we do know that they have the capability to transfer information from one sense to another sense. This requires the ability to picture something in one's head." The bees think in pictures.

The Man Who Studied Bees

Born in 1867, Charles Henry Turner was the first African American to earn a PhD in zoology. After that, he went on to publish seventy research papers in prestigious journals, including *Science*, but discrimination against Black people prevented him from being hired as a university professor. He spent his life working as a high school teacher and continuing his own research on insects.

Turner proved that honeybees can see and hear and that they are capable of learning. He believed that bees create "memory pictures of their environment" that allow them to communicate with each other and navigate. The memory pictures bees use to navigate back to their hives are like the way people use visual landmarks to remember how to get from place to place. For example, if you tell yourself to turn left at the Dairy Queen to get to school, your mind is using a memory picture to help you navigate. He was able to show that animals modified or changed their behavior based on experience. They learned. Turner's pioneering research continues to inform our ideas about animal behavior to this day.

Researcher Jessie Peissig found that pigeons group shapes into categories, a skill that was previously thought to be something only humans can do. And Shigeru Watanabe came to similar conclusions when he found that pigeons could be taught to tell a Monet painting from a Picasso. It's likely this skill is adaptive in order for the pigeons to identify their surroundings. All mammals and birds know where their den or nest is located, and they use visual thinking to remember where it is, as well as to locate food sources. Squirrels and birds also can remember where they have hidden food *and* how long it has been hidden. Jays know that delicious worms rot faster than nuts. They know that they must go back and eat the worms more quickly than the nuts, just as we refrigerate perishables such as dairy and leave the Oreo cookies in the pantry for weeks at a time.

Nature vs. Nurture: The Animal Edition

In the 1950s and 1960s, the study of animal behavior was dominated by two approaches: the study of animals in their natural environment (ethology) and the study of animals in the laboratory (behaviorism). But while ethologists and behaviorists disagreed on *how* to study animals, they both agreed that animals didn't have emotions. They just couldn't imagine that any creature that couldn't speak could have thoughts or feelings. Instead, they chose to study the animals' behaviors and actions.

The ethologists believed that animal behavior was controlled by genetics and instincts, and the behaviorists believed that it was controlled by the environment—sort of like the nature-versus-nurture argument that we discussed earlier, but in this case focused on animals. The two schools of thought both believed they could study behavior objectively, the behaviorists via lab tests and the ethologists by observing an animal's behavior in nature. Konrad Lorenz, a pioneer of ethology and a Nobel Prize winner, believed that animals should not be held "prisoner" in order to be studied. He felt that the only way to learn about them was through close observation and over time. This was a point of view widely popularized through the work of Jane Goodall, who studied chimpanzees in the wild. Less well known is Anne Dagg, who chose to study giraffes in the wild.

The Woman Who Loved Giraffes

As a child, Anne Dagg fell in love with giraffes at the Toronto Zoo, so much so that when she grew up, she chose to study them. Unable to find governmental or academic support, Dagg disguised her gender and appealed to a rancher in Africa whose cattle ranch was in close proximity to the Kruger National Park, home to a large giraffe population. She received an invitation from him and, at the age of twenty-three, traveled to Africa on her own. When her gender was revealed, the rancher allowed

The pioneering researcher Anne Dagg observed giraffes in the wild.

her to stay in exchange for work in the office. Kruger National Park became her laboratory. Dagg kept extensive notes about what the giraffes ate (she categorized every leaf and tree) and how they walked, ran, played, fought, and mated. After a giraffe was killed, she recorded everything from the length of its intestines—which she dried on a clothesline—to their contents, studying what plants the animal had ingested, as well as testing for parasites. The legacy of her pioneering work on the study of animals in the wild, and giraffes in particular, continues today through the Anne Innis Dagg Foundation, which works to protect giraffes and their habitats.

Today, it's mainly believed that behaviors such as eating, mating, and nurturing their young are innate, as well as animal-specific behaviors such as nectar-seeking in honeybees, web-spinning in spiders, and nest-building in birds. For example, a weaverbird will always build the same type of distinctive woven nest, even without seeing an example of one. They are simply born knowing how to make them.

Weaverbirds weave elaborate nests. They have an innate instinctual ability to build these nests.

How animals fight is innate. When bulls fight, they butt heads, but when horses fight, they rear up and strike with their front hooves. And even highly domesticated animals have abilities that are specific to their species. A dog, for instance, will perform a bow when it wants to play, and domestic turkeys will fan their tails to attract mates. (A barnful of male turkeys once displayed their fanned tails to me, though I am hardly a suitable mate!)

Animals can also learn new behaviors that they are not born with. Horses, for instance, can easily learn to be ridden. And we have all seen dogs that have been taught to roll over or play catch. Playing Frisbee is not a skill a dog is born with—obviously it has to be learned.

Animals can also plan. Researcher Nicola Clayton proved this with an experiment I like to call "the cheap hotel and the expensive hotel." During the day, a scrub jay had free rein of two compartments, or "hotels." At night he would be locked in one of the hotels, but he would only receive breakfast after spending the night in the "expensive hotel." Scrub jays quickly learned to store more of their food in the cheap hotel, having learned they wouldn't be served a complimentary breakfast as they had been at the expensive hotel. It's the equivalent of packing sandwiches when you know there won't be any food available on a hike. They planned for the possibility of being locked in the cheap hotel.

But even as scientists began noting that animals can learn, B. F. Skinner, a behaviorist, strongly said that they don't think or feel. He summed up his thoughts succinctly in this 1977 statement in *Behaviorism*, titled "Why I Am Not a Cognitive Psychologist": "I see no evidence of an inner world of mental life." Remarkably, he wasn't just talking about animals either. He believed that humans also had no inner life. According to Skinner, both people and animals are controlled by two simple forces: rewards and punishments. He wrote that free will is a fantasy, and that "the 'emotions' are excellent examples of the fictional causes to which we commonly attribute behavior."

The Skinner Box

B. F. Skinner invented the Skinner box, a test used to explore animal behaviors. This method is still widely used in animal research today. In the first boxes that Skinner created, rats or pigeons were placed inside and shown two levers. If they pushed one lever, they would get a food pellet—a reward. If they pushed the other, they would get an electric shock—a punishment. Not surprisingly, the animals learned to press the food levers. Skinner showed that animals learn to modify behavior through rewards and punishments, which he called operant conditioning. And it functions the same in humans. If the teacher tells a noisy group of students that they can't go outside for recess until they settle down, they learn quickly to sit quietly in their chairs. Punishment: losing precious time on the playground. Reward: freedom!

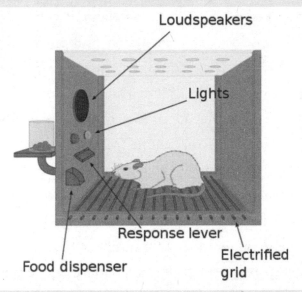

Skinner tested his learning theories in an apparatus he developed that came to be known as a Skinner box. This version of the box shows two lights and one response lever that animals can push depending on which light is on.

I got the opportunity to meet and speak with Dr. Skinner in the 1960s, after I had written a letter to him. When I had a chance, I asked him about the brain and how it works. Skinner replied, "We don't need to learn about the brain because we have operant conditioning." Years later, I heard that, after Skinner had a stroke, he admitted that maybe we do need to learn about the brain after all.

Animal specialists Keller and Marian Breland disputed Skinner's ideas in their 1961 paper "The Misbehavior of Organisms." The pair had studied under Skinner and worked as research assistants in his lab. In the paper, they showed that his ideas about reward and punishment didn't quite play out, because "operant conditioning" could be overridden by an animal's instincts. A carnival novelty that I once witnessed at the Arizona State Fair backed up their findings. When a hen pecked the keys on a toy piano, it got a reward. This worked well because pecking is instinctual to hens. It's what they do naturally. In another attempt to train an animal, I learned that trying to get a raccoon to put coins into a small box didn't work at all. Raccoons like to wash their food. When trainers gave the coins to the raccoons, the raccoons rubbed the coins, attempting to perform their instinctual food-washing behavior, and refused to drop them in the box. No matter how much food it was given, it refused to change its instinctive ways.

The Brelands went on to set up a business to commercially train animals, and over the years, they trained more than eight thousand animals for television ads, circuses, movies, and television shows. The animal training programs used today at popular theme parks such as SeaWorld and Busch Gardens are based on methods and ideas that the Brelands pioneered more than fifty years ago.

Because the Brelands operated a business instead of researching at a university, their work was often dismissed as unscientific. But their observations resonated with me. I know that animals are about more than just levers, food pellets, and electrical shocks, the same way we are.

The Animal Brain

In the 1990s, new developments in MRI technology allowed scientists to look at animal brains in more detail than they had ever been able to before, and it led to a robust scientific debate about animals and whether they have consciousness. For an animal to have consciousness, it must have a complex brain and nervous system. If you don't have a nervous system, then you don't have a brain. And if you don't have a brain, then you can't be conscious.

Let's start at the most basic, simple creatures and work our way up. Clams, oysters, and maggots, for instance, are not conscious. Their behavior is the result of reflexes. If you touch an oyster, it will close its shell. They don't close their shell because they don't like you, or because they are having a bad day. They are just closing because that's what they do. It's a reflex, not an emotional response.

The next step up is the flatworm. Flatworms are just a bit more complicated than the clam and have in their heads the beginnings of neurons that connect to one another. These centralized hubs are the keys to consciousness in more complex animals. But in the flatworm, they are still far too simple to foster consciousness.

The next stage is being able to see. All mammals, reptiles, spiders, and insects have eyes that can see images with some degree of clarity. Though ants and wasps, for instance, are not able to see as well as we can, they rely on vision for some important tasks, including using landmarks as navigational tools.

As we continue to go up toward more and more complexity, it's important to note that size is not a factor here. Have you ever heard anyone insult someone by saying, "He's such a birdbrain"? The logic of the insult is that birds are small, so their brains are small; therefore, they must be stupid. So, if I call you a birdbrain, I'm saying you're stupid, too. But the logic doesn't hold. Birds have highly complicated brains with a tremendous amount of processing power for their small size. Their brains are sort of like a powerful smart-phone, which is small enough to fit in your pocket but can do just as much as desktop computers. Perhaps, in order to allow birds to fly, evolution made sure their brains were light, while still powerful.

Now let's skip up to the highest-level mammals. Many mammals, such as people, dogs, elephants, and apes, have brains with complex centralized hubs that can take in information from multiple sources and connect them to one another. You could compare the hubs in their brains to an airport, where planes come in from different cities and meet up. In animal brains, the "airplanes" are different types of information, like memories, senses, or emotions, and the "airport" is the part of the brain that is the centralized hub that collects and organizes all the information. To continue the airport analogy, the human brain would be a huge airport, such as Atlanta, Georgia, or Dallas Fort Worth, Texas, and a dog's brain would be like a small regional airport.

So, when a tiger smells its prey with its nose, that scent is one type of information. And when it remembers the smell from the last time it had a snack, that's a second type of information, a memory. The hub in the tiger's brain is complex enough to take both the memory and the scent, combine them, and let the tiger understand more about its potential meal.

We are finally now at the very top level, and the brain of the most complicated creatures: humans.

When people ask me what the difference is between us humans and animals, I put my hand on my head and say, "The size of our computing power!" The huge number of circuits in our cerebral cortex is many times larger than that of any other species. By way of comparison, the human brain has 16.3 billion cortical neurons, and the elephant has only 5.6 billion. Elephants are extremely intelligent compared to many other animals, but we humans are still smarter. And since our brain systems are more complex, our consciousness is more complex, too. That's why I was able to write this book, but a chimpanzee, smart as he might be, was not. But they still do think, even if they can't write books, and scientists continue to explore how, using tests like the "mirror test."

The Mirror Test

When an animal looks at its own reflection in a mirror, does it recognize that it is seeing itself, or does it think it is looking at a different animal? In the view of many scientists, this is the perfect test, the gold standard of measuring consciousness. A creature that can pass the mirror test is considered to have self-awareness.

Psychologist Gordon Gallup developed the mirror self-recognition (MSR) test to explore this further. He sedated chimps and painted a red mark on their bodies. Then when they were awake, he put them in front of a mirror, where they could see the red mark. If the chimps investigated where the mark had been applied to their bodies, they recognized that the image in the mirror reflected themselves, and so were considered to have self-awareness.

When an animal takes the mirror test, they often look around the mirror to see if someone else is hiding behind it. They sometimes attempt to interact with their reflection, thinking it is another creature. Sometimes they will try to make friends with it, while other times they see it as a threat and start acting aggressively toward it.

But as they get to the next step, they become more interested in the reflection and begin to test it by going in and out of view. Finally, once they've realized that "Hey! That's me!" they will begin to investigate their faces and other body parts. Dolphins and elephants in some of these mirror studies will bend into weird positions to examine themselves. As a child, I remember doing the same thing in the three-way mirrors in clothing-store dressing rooms. Another time I tried to figure out why the writing on my T-shirt appeared backward in the mirror. I discovered that it was still backward even when I switched the side with the writing to my back.

The mirror test has been one way to measure animal consciousness.

Many of Gallup's chimps passed the mirror test. But dogs did not. If you have a dog, you've probably noticed that upon seeing its reflection, it will either bark or not react to it at all. It doesn't recognize its reflection as being itself. To date, the small group of animals that have been able to pass the miror test includes chimps, bonobos, gorillas, orangutans, elephants, dolphins, and magpies. Happy, the elephant from the court case described earlier, had also passed the mirror test.

Jonathan Birch and his colleagues Alexandra Schnell and Nicola Clayton have said that some of the animals who can't pass the mirror test should still be added to the list of animals who possess "some form of consciousness." They argue that the reason dogs do not pass the mirror test is likely because their way of socializing is through smell and hearing, with vision a distant third.

Human babies can pass the mirror test at about one and a half to two years old. Their more complicated emotions start to develop at this age as well, such as embarrassment, envy, and empathy. Later, humans develop even more complex emotions, such as guilt and pride.

In addition to self-awareness, some argue that the true proof of consciousness is the ability to problem-solve and use tools. Researcher Gavin Hunt observed that wild crows make tools and use them to reach food. And when scientist A. M. P. von Bayern gave crows pieces of wooden dowels, syringe barrels, and plungers, the crows figured out how to assemble them into even longer tools.

When Jane Goodall first observed that chimps used sticks as tools to fish for termites, many people did not want to believe it. Until then, scientists had believed that what separated humans from chimps was (1) our ability to make and use tools and (2) speech. Goodall also discovered that chimps use leaves as sponges to soak up water to drink, use rocks to crack open nuts and gourds, and sharpen sticks to use as spears.

Author Simon Baron-Cohen thinks these facts don't matter much and disagrees. In his book *The Pattern Seekers,* he says, "Chimpanzees and humans split from our common ancestor eight million years ago, so they've had as long as we have had to develop a capacity

NASA sent Ham the chimpanzee, our closest relative, before sending a human astronaut into orbit.

to invent complex tools, like a bicycle, a paintbrush, or a bow-and-arrow." And since they haven't, he's unimpressed with their abilities and thinking.

Yet when NASA needed an animal to send into space before trying it out with a human, they turned to our closest relative, the chimpanzee. If a chimp could survive leaving the earth's atmosphere, it was likely that an astronaut would be able to survive as well. Eric Betz in *Discover* points out that while dogs had been used as passengers, "NASA needed a test subject with the intelligence and dexterity to prove it could operate a spacecraft." And on January 31, 1961, Ham became the first chimp to travel into space, aboard the Mercury-Redstone rocket, paving the way for the space program.

The First Hot Air Balloon

Ham wasn't the first animal to test whether a flight would be safe for humans. In 1783, brothers Joseph-Michel and Jacques-Étienne Montgolfier discovered that a large balloon would float if it was filled with hot air. After presenting their discovery in the small French town where they grew up, they presented their hot air balloon again near Paris, this time with three living passengers: a duck, a rooster, and a sheep named Montauciel (Climb-to-the-Sky). The animals survived, and a month later, the Montgolfiers sent a human up in a balloon.

Do Animals Have Emotions?

While the idea that at least some animals have consciousness has become more and more accepted in the scientific community, recognition of animal emotion continues to prove a thornier road.

Nobel Prize–winning zoologist Konrad Lorenz believed that animals have emotions. He is well known for his ideas about "imprinting," a concept he claims stemmed from when he was a child and given a day-old duckling as a pet. Since the baby duck had no mother to follow, it followed him around instead. This experience informed Lorenz's later studies, in which he explored the bonds that are formed between newborns and their caregivers in the first weeks of life, which he called imprinting and attachment.

Anne Dagg, in her observations of giraffes, noticed that they would often keep visiting the site where their relatives had passed away. She concluded that their actions showed that "such emotion is more common in the wild

Konrad Lorenz was awarded the Nobel Prize for his ideas of animal "imprinting," or bonding.

than we appreciate." And according to Iain Douglas-Hamilton and his colleagues from the organization Save the Elephants, elephants will attempt to lift a dying elephant back to its feet when it can no longer stand, and then many different elephant families will visit the body after death. This seems to suggest that elephants also feel and mourn the loss of their family members.

Frans de Waal has dedicated his life to the study of primate behavior and has been a lifelong advocate for the recognition of animal emotion. Often going against the opinions of the scientific community, he writes, "Science doesn't like imprecision, which is why when it comes to animal emotions, it is often at odds with the view of the general public." Most of us who have pets would agree with Montaigne: we have no doubt our cats and dogs and horses have feelings. It's the university professors, de Waal says, who balk. De Waal also believes that our prejudice for verbal communication makes it hard to understand that animals feel emotions, since they can't speak. Researcher Michael Fanselow agrees: "In my opinion, their approaches suffer from the human tendency to glorify verbal report over all other measures."

I've noticed this, too. Many scientists I've met who are verbal thinkers have trouble believing that animals can think and have emotions. Since many scientists themselves think in words and through speech, the idea that other creatures could think in sensory-based information and emotions is foreign to them.

But it's their very lack of language that makes animals such fascinating creatures to learn from, including how they think and accomplish tasks without using speech. Homing pigeons can find their way home without using Google Maps, Waze, or even reading street signs.

Our human ancestors might have thought visually before they learned how to speak. A recent study by Dana Michelle Cataldo revealed how our ancestors might have created stone blades before they could talk or write. The participants in her study, who didn't know anything about toolmaking, were divided into two groups. An expert flintknapper (someone skilled in making knife-like tools from stones) showed the first group how to make the tool, using words to explain the process as well. For the second group, the same expert demonstrated the process but, instead of using words, he used only nonverbal cues, like pointing and other hand motions, sort of like you would in a game of charades. Participants in the no-words group performed better at learning the task. This highlights how nonverbal learning and thinking may have played a significant role in early human achievement, an idea worth thinking about as we consider the ways animals think and feel, too.

To me, it's obvious that animals have emotions. Dogs, for example, can get upset when their owners leave them home alone all day. When I take a midday walk through my neighborhood, I can hear dogs whining and barking. Some will chew up shoes or slippers if they are left alone. I know a graphic designer whose cat pooped on his pillow when he went away for a night. Just like there are some grumpy people and some pleasant people, different animals have different temperaments. Some dogs are content to sleep all day while their owners are gone and then greet them warmly when they get home, while others are not.

Scientist Jaak Panksepp described emotions in animals in seven distinct categories:

- Seeking (exploration): This is the basic impulse to explore. When animals feel this, they investigate and make sense of their environment.
- Rage (anger): Critical for survival, rage can motivate an animal to fight off an attacking predator.
- Fear (anxiety): Fear motivates an animal to avoid dangerous traps, being attacked, and other risks.
- Lust (sex drive): Lust is a feeling that greatly increases in both people and animals at puberty. It motivates them to reproduce.
- Care (nurturing): Nearly all people and warm-blooded animals have feelings that motivate them to nurture their young. This is sometimes called the maternal instinct.
- Panic (grief/sadness): Different from fear, this is an example of separation distress, such as what a mother animal might feel when separated from its young. When a dog is left home alone and chews up the house, that is also due to separation distress.
- Play (social joy): All young mammals, including human children, are motivated to play. Play helps them learn how to socially interact and develop intellectually.

There are also situations where more than one emotional system is involved in motivating behavior. Panksepp originally studied emotions by electrically stimulating regions of the brain that controlled emotions. Today, scientists use less invasive methods such as fMRI and PET scans. New fMRI methods are being developed to enable more precise localization of where emotions in the brain originate.

One of the scientists doing this work is Gregory Berns. He wanted to scan dogs' brains, so he trained the dogs to voluntarily enter an MRI scanner and lie very still. He declined to use restraints on the animals because he believed it would violate their rights. The dogs could leave the scanner at any time. Using the dogs who could tolerate the MRI, he recorded their brain activity while showing them videos. The first showed food being given to a (very realistic looking) fake dog, and the second showed the food being put into a bucket. The part of the dogs' brains called the amygdala showed greater activity when the fake dog was fed than when food was put into the bucket. Since the dogs only reacted when other dogs were fed, they may have been feeling something like jealousy. Berns also found that certain dogs preferred verbal praise from their owners over a treat. They were demonstrating an emotional connection to their owner: friendship.

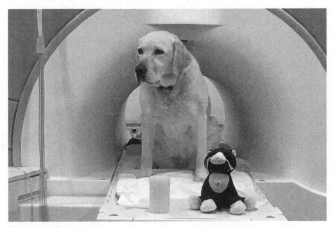

Gregory Berns trained dogs to lie still in the MRI to learn more about emotions and their ability to understand words.

Another scientist, Mylène Quervel-Chaumette, has looked at the feelings and relationships between dogs that lived together. The dogs were separated from their housemates and then played different recordings. The first recording played the sounds of the dog they lived with. The second played the sounds of a strange dog, and the third played random computer-generated noises. When the dogs heard their friends, they had stronger responses, like tucking their tail between their legs or whining. They were showing that they missed their friends.

Scientists have found clear examples of octopuses showing emotions, too. In the 2020 documentary *My Octopus Teacher*, naturalist Craig Foster discovers an octopus in a South African kelp forest. At first, the octopus disappears out of sight upon his arrival. But Foster keeps returning, keeping a respectful distance. Over time, the octopus develops an interest in her human visitor and eventually comes closer. Near the end of the film, the octopus allows Foster to hold her. The octopus feels safe; she has formed a friendship with him.

On the other side of this argument is neuroscientist Joseph LeDoux. He has said that animals don't feel fear. When we see an animal in distress, they are just showing their instinct to protect themselves from danger, not a true emotion. In his 2015 book *Anxious*, he went so far as to claim that all animal reactions are merely survival instincts. I heard that later, at an International Society for Applied Ethology conference, LeDoux was asked why he didn't feel that animals have true emotional lives and feelings. He stated that he thought, as a person, that they had true emotions, but as a scientist, he was not sure. It's possible that verbal thinkers like LeDoux just cannot consider that animals have another way of thinking and feeling.

In the early 1990s, animal scientists were not allowed to use the words "fear" or "emotion." Scientists were not supposed to think that animals showed distress. Scientists were not supposed to think that animals had feelings. If you did, you would get accused of being unobjective. That was the worst possible insult you could ever say to a scientist, so describing any emotion in an animal was taboo. Instead, I used terms such as "behavioral agitation" to describe when an animal showed distress. When I was just dealing with ideas, that approach made some sense to me. But all that changed when I stepped onto my first cattle plant and placed my hands against the side of a steer. It was like a current ran through me. I could instantly tell whether the animal was anxious, angry, agitated, or relaxed. I didn't need more proof than that. I knew in my bones that animals have feelings just like my own.

More than twenty-five years ago, in my book *Thinking in Pictures*, I predicted that science would catch up with my thinking on this someday. Today, I am pleased to report that it seems it finally has. There are hundreds of researchers around the world studying animals' emotions in laboratories, on farms, and in the wild. Doreen Cabrera is one. She reviewed thirty-six personality studies in a variety of mammals, birds, reptiles, and insects and concluded that they all show different types of emotional traits, such as boldness, fear, and curiosity. Emotion has taken its rightful place alongside genetics and environment as a major influence on animal behavior. This is a huge development.

I am not the only human to have made these types of connections with animals. The best horse trainers I have observed can train a wild colt to be ridden within two hours. One of these trainers, Ray Hunt, was hopeless at explaining what he did. The best he could manage was that he tries to "get in tune with the horse." What he was trying to say is that when he works with a horse, he strives to understand its feelings and connect to it.

Cattle whisperers also connect to animals on an emotional level. Bud Williams and Burt Smith are two of the best that I've seen. They can get a group of cattle to gather into the center of a field, drawing them out from the edges of the pasture, even from behind bushes, and they don't do this with bullhorns, a bunch of screaming cowhands, jeeps, or helicopters. Instead, they walk back and forth in a zigzag pattern on the edge of the herd. Their walking pattern triggers an instinctual behavior in the cows, and the herd draws together. For this to work, Bud and Burt both need to be highly sensitive to the feelings of the herd, otherwise the cattle will scatter.

When I asked Burt to explain how he and Bud do what they do, he responded by drawing a diagram at his kitchen table, with arrows for the cows. It looked like the diagonal lines in a parking lot. This confirmed for me that he is a visual thinker. Like Ray, he could not verbally explain how he did what he did. But he was an expert at it.

The same is true of many animal handlers. They make emotional, wordless connections with animals. This is something I've noticed we have in common: we all think in pictures, and privilege smells, sounds, and touch over verbal communication. Words are not our primary means of communication. For verbal thinkers, this type of connection is extremely difficult to understand. Their focus on words and abstract ideas can distance them from picking up on the cues animals use to communicate their emotions and needs.

I can still recall a story that Ron Kilgour, an animal behavior scientist, shared with me about a lion who was transported in a crate on a plane. His owner had decided to place a pillow inside the crate along with the lion. When the plane landed and the crate was opened, the lion was dead, and the pillow was gone. What happened? Sadly, this isn't a whodunit, mystery, or riddle. The lion had eaten the pillow. The story brought home to me how verbal thinking can make it difficult to understand the needs of an animal. To me, it's obvious that a lion would need straw spread out on the hard metal floor of the crate, not a pillow. But the owner couldn't imagine the animal's needs from the animal's point of view, so he gave the lion the wrong thing entirely.

Because I understand animals, and because I deeply believe they have emotions like fear and pain, I care about them. Seeing animals suffer in pain hurts me because I can visualize how they feel. This is why, over the course of my career, I've pushed and advocated on their behalf.

Why I'm Not a Vegetarian

If I love animals so much, why do I think it's okay for people to eat them? Why do I help design slaughterhouses? Why aren't I a vegetarian?

It's because I respect nature for what it is. Lions kill antelope, warthogs, zebra, and giraffes for food. Some sharks will kill just about anything that swims—tuna, dolphins, seals, and sea lions—for food. Death in nature is often harsh and cruel. But it's nature. Humans are part of that chain. We eat animals for food. But that doesn't mean we should be cruel about it. We should give animals lives worth living and be responsible stewards of the animals we have domesticated for our food. Twenty percent of the earth's habitable land is too arid to raise crops. When rotational grazing is done right, it can improve the soil.

So, yes, I'll enjoy the occasional steak and fries. But I make sure that it comes from a ranch that treats nature and animals with respect.

Ten years ago, I still remember pondering whether to speak out while making a six-hour drive to lecture at a livestock meeting. I had become aware that some cattle were suffering from heat stress and lameness, and I was nervous. If I spoke out about it, it might hurt my career. But as I drove, I looked outside my car windows at the pastures of cattle and knew that I had no choice. I visualized the animals and their pain. It was my duty to tell cattle producers about the problems that had to be fixed. I spoke out, and I got a lot of pushback from the livestock industry about it. But it was worth it. I strongly believed then, and still believe today, that humans must be responsible stewards of the animals they have domesticated for food. Today when I visit a slaughter plant, I still get angry when I see problems that cause cattle unnecessary anxiety, pain, or suffering. Our culture has a split personality where animals are concerned.

On the one hand, we dress our dogs up in baby clothes and feed them human food. In New York City, I've seen Chihuahuas with ribbons in their hair being pushed around in baby carriages. At the same time, we also abandon our dogs and/or confine them to small apartments for many hours each day. They seldom get to participate in natural dog behavior, such as socializing with other dogs and sniffing the outdoors to learn what the other dogs are doing. Many also suffer from separation anxiety when they are left home alone all day. Both approaches—giving animals ribbons or trapping them in an apartment alone—show that too many humans just don't "get" their animals. If they did, they would know that dogs don't want ribbons, or isolation. Instead, dogs are most happy when they are allowed to roam their neighborhoods. Dogs are much happier hanging out with other dogs than playing with toys all by themselves. It is our responsibility to give animals lives worth living.

Imagine if we made the world as hospitable for visual thinkers as it is for verbal thinkers. If we didn't assume that we all perceived and processed our surroundings the same way, we could tap into and harness so much more brain power than we have.

Throughout graduate school, I was able to adopt the supposedly objective stance of the scientist. It made a lot of sense. All that changed when I touched a steer at my first cattle plant and realized animals have emotions. Some, like chimps and dolphins, also have self-awareness. Others feel through their senses, like the elephants who mourn for their herd mates when they die. They may not have words to tell us about their feelings, but I believe animals have consciousness. They are visual thinkers.

If we can come together, we can create a safer, more inclusive, more advanced society that will lead in manufacturing, technology, and finding solutions to the challenges of our rapidly changing and complex world. Someone recently asked me if I thought we really can change the world. I do. One place to start is understanding that we need all kinds of thinkers. Imagine how different a world it could be.

Acknowledgments

I FIRST WANT TO RECOGNIZE ALL THE TEACHERS WHO HELPED me to have a successful life. I had no speech until age four and I am autistic. My education started with Miss Reynolds, my speech teacher. I was enrolled in her early childhood program at age two and a half. My mother always encouraged my ability in art and pushed me to try new things by giving me choices. Everett Ladd, the principal at the Dedham Country Day School, worked as a team with my mother on my elementary school education. They both made sure that the rules were consistent between home and school. By age eight, I was still not able to read and Mrs. Alice Dietsch, my third grade teacher, was really concerned. To help me to learn reading, my mother taught me with phonics and we read an interesting book out loud.

High school was a disaster of bullying and teasing After I got thrown out of a large high school for throwing a book at a girl who called me names, I went to Hampshire Country School. They had both horses and dairy cattle. Horses became my life and Henry Patey, the headmaster, put me to work cleaning stalls. Horseback riding was one of the activities where I had friends through shared interests. Another super-important teacher was Mr. William Carlock, my science teacher. He challenged me with interesting projects and showed me that studying would provide a pathway to becoming a scientist. Almost overnight, I pulled my grades up. Having a goal got me motivated to study. When I was in college, I still visited with Mr. Carlock. He taught me important skills, such as learning to use scientific databases. I also wish to thank Mr.

Norb Dion, my math teacher, who taught freshman college math. When I had problems with math, he tutored me in his office. Both Frank DiPietro, the president, and Clifford Coles, the dean of Franklin Pierce College, saw that I had abilities and they allowed me to enter the college on probation. I graduated second in my class as the salutatorian.

Other people who were important mentors were Ann Brecheen on her ranch in Arizona and Phillip Stiles, the Introductory Animal Science teacher at Arizona State University. Dr. Stiles helped me get started in animal science. In the 1970s when I was getting my career started, there were some outstanding people in the Arizona cattle industry who mentored me. I had the opportunity to design facilities for them. They were Tom Rohrer, Norb Goscowitz, and Harley Winkelman at the Swift plant. Other industry leaders who encouraged me were Sam McElhany, owner of McElhany Cattle Company, and Ted Gilbert, Manager of the Red River Feedlot. Another person who helped get my career started was Jim Uhl, owner of a small construction business. He recognized my abilities, built my early projects, and showed me how to start my own business.

Entering the cattle industry in the 1970s as a woman was not easy. I had to make myself really good at my design work. The top people who owned the cattle feedlots were good to me. It was the foremen and middle managers who did not want a woman invading their turf. I encourage students to find mentors and teachers. They will help students go into careers that they will love.

Finally, I want to acknowledge all the people who made this book possible. They were Jill Santopolo, my editor, and Ann D. Koffsky, who wrote the initial draft of the adaptation of *Visual Thinking*. Betsy Lerner is also thanked for her tireless work on final revisions and editing. Additional thanks and gratitude to Cheryl Miller for her help at every stage, to Gregory Berns for permission to use photos from his research, and to Jack Petersen and Want Chyi for their editorial assistance.

Bibliography

Selected References from *Visual Thinking*

Introduction

Chomsky, Noam. *Syntactic Structures*. Eastford, CT: Martino Fine Books, 2015.

Descartes, René. *Meditations on First Philosophy: With Selections from the Objections and Replies*. 2nd ed. Translated and edited by John Cottingham. Cambridge, UK: Cambridge University Press, 2017.

Frener & Reifer. "Steve Jobs Theater." Accessed August 7, 2021. frener-reifer.com /news-en/steve-jobs-theater.

Grandin, Temple. *Thinking in Pictures and Other Reports from My Life with Autism*. New York: Doubleday, 1995.

Grandin, Temple. *Thinking in Pictures: My Life with Autism*. Expanded edition. New York: Vintage, 2006.

Kozhevnikov, Maria, Mary Hegarty, and Richard E. Mayer. "Revising the Visualizer-Verbalizer Dimension: Evidence for Two Types of Visualizers." *Cognition and Instruction* 20, no. 1 (2002): 47–77.

Kozhevnikov, Maria, Stephen Kosslyn, and Jennifer Shephard. "Spatial versus Object Visualizers: A New Characterization of Visual Cognitive Style." *Memory & Cognition* 33, no. 4 (June 2005): 710–726.

Sedak. "Apple Park, Cupertino California, 2,500 Glass Units in Façade." Accessed August 7, 2021. sedak.com/en/references/facades/apple-park-cupertino-use.

Chapter One: What Is Visual Thinking?

Alfonsi, Sharyn. "Meet the Blind Piano Player Who's So Good, Scientists Are Studying Him." *60 Minutes*. CBS News. December 27, 2020. cbsnews.com/news/matthew -whitaker-blind-jazz-pianist-18-years-old-60-minutes-2020-12-27.

Bainbridge, Wilma A, et al. "Quantifying Aphantasia through Drawing: Those without Visual Imagery Show Deficits in Object but Not Spatial Memory." *Cortex* 135 (February 2021): 159–172.

Blajenkova, Olessia, Maria Kozhevnikov, and Michael A. Motes. "Object-Spatial Imagery: A New Self-Report Imagery Questionnaire." *Applied Cognitive Psychology* 20, no. 2 (March 2006): 239–263. doi.org/10.1002/acp.1182.

Blazhenkova, Olesya, and Maria Kozhevnikov. "Creative Processes during a Collaborative Drawing Task in Teams of Different Specializations" *Creative Education* 11, no. 9 (September 2020): 1751–1775.

Blazhenkova, Olesya, and Maria Kozhevnikov. "Types of Creativity and Visualization in Teams of Different Educational Specialization." *Creativity Research Journal* 28, no. 2 (2016): 123–135.

Chabris, Christopher F., et al. "Spatial and Object Visualization Cognitive Styles: Validation Studies in 3,800 Individuals." *Group Brain Technical Report* 2 (2006): 1–20.

Cropley, David H., and James C. Kaufman. "The Siren Song of Aesthetics? Domain Differences and Creativity in Engineering and Design." *Proceedings of the Institution of Mechanical Engineers, Part C: Journal of Mechanical Engineering Science* 233, no. 2 (January 2019): 451–464.

Dean, Josh. "Making Marines into MacGyvers." *Bloomberg Businessweek*, September 20, 2018, 48–55.

Dolgin, Elie. "A Loop of Faith." *Nature* 544 (April 2017): 284–286.

Gardner, Howard. *Multiple Intelligences: New Horizons in Theory and Practice.* Revised edition. New York: Basic Books, 2006.

Grandin, Temple. "How Does Visual Thinking Work in the Mind of a Person with Autism? A Personal Account." *Philosophical Transactions of the Royal Society B: Biological Sciences* 364, no 1522 (May 2009): 1437–1442.

Höffler, Tim N., Marta Koć-Januchta, and Detlev Leutner. "More Evidence for Three Types of Cognitive Style: Validating the Object-Spatial Imagery and Verbal Questionnaire Using Eye Tracking When Learning with Texts and Pictures." *Applied Cognitive Psychology* 31, no. 1 (January/February 2017): 109–115. doi.org/10.1002/acp.3300.

Khatchadourian, Raffi. "The Elusive Peril of Space Junk." *New Yorker*, September 21, 2020.

Khatchadourian, Raffi. "The Trash Nebula." *New Yorker*, September 28, 2020.

Koć-Januchta, Marta, et al. "Visualizers versus Verbalizers: Effects of Cognitive Style on Learning with Texts and Pictures—An Eye-Tracking Study." *Computers in Human Behavior* 68 (March 2017): 170–179. doi.org/10.1016/j.chb.2016.11.028.

Kozhevnikov, Maria, Olesya Blazhenkova, and Michael Becker. "Trade-Off in Object versus Spatial Visualization Abilities: Restriction in the Development of Visual-Processing Resources." *Psychonomic Bulletin & Review* 17, no. 1 (February 2010): 29–35.

Masataka, Nobuo. "Were Musicians as Well as Artists in the Ice Age Caves Likely with Autism Spectrum Disorder? A Neurodiversity Hypothesis." In *The Origins of Language Revisited*, edited by Nobuo Masataka, 323–345. Singapore: Springer, 2020. doi.org/10.1007/978-981-15-4250-3_9.

Mottron, Laurent. "The Power of Autism." *Nature* 479 (November 2011): 33–35.

Mottron, Laurent, et al. "Enhanced Perceptual Functioning in Autism: An Update, and Eight Principles of Autistic Perception." *Journal of Autism and*

Developmental Disorders 36, no 1 (January 2006): 27–43.

Park, Clara Claiborne. *Exiting Nirvana: A Daughter's Life with Autism*. New York: Little, Brown, 2001.

Putt, Shelby S., Alexander D. Woods, and Robert G. Franciscus. "The Role of Verbal Interaction during Experimental Bifacial Stone Tool Manufacture." *Lithic Technology* 39, no. 2 (2014): 96–112.

Sikela, J. M., and V. B. Searles Quick. "Genomic Trade-Offs: Are Autism and Schizophrenia the Steep Price of the Human Brain?" *Human Genetics* 137, no. 1 (January 2018): 1–13.

Silberman, Steve. "The Geek Syndrome." *Wired*, December 1, 2001. wired.com /2001/12/aspergers.

Sutton, Mike. "Snakes, Sausages and Structural Formulae." *Chemistry World*, October 8, 2015. chemistryworld.com/features/snakes-sausages-and -structural-formulae/9038.article.

Thaler, Lore. "Echolocation May Have Real-Life Advantages for Blind People: An Analysis of Survey Data." *Frontiers in Physiology* 4 (May 2013). doi.org/10.3389 /fphys.2013.00098.

Vance, Ashlee. *Elon Musk: Tesla, SpaceX, and the Quest for a Fantastic Future*. New York: Ecco, 2015.

Vazquez, Carlos M., II. "Technology Book Camp Aims to Upgrade Okinawa-Based Marines' Problem-Solving Skills." *Stars and Stripes*, March 26, 2019.

Watanabe, Shigeru, Junko Sakamoto, and Masumi Wakita. "Pigeons' Discrimination of Paintings by Monet and Picasso." *Journal of the Experimental Analysis of Behavior* 63, no. 2 (March 1995): 165–174.

Weintraub, Karen. "Temple Grandin on How the Autistic 'Think Different.'" *USA Today*, May 1, 2013. usatoday.comnwes/nation/2013/05/01/autism-temple -grandin-brain/2122455.

Zeman, Adam, et al. "Phantasia—The Psychological Significance of Lifelong

Visual Imagery Vividness Extremes." *Cortex* 130 (September 2020): 426–440. doi:10.1016/j.cortex.2020.04.003.

Chapter Two: Screened Out

Asmika, Asmika, et al. "Autistic Children Are More Responsive to Tactile Sensory Stimulus." *Iranian Journal of Child Neurology* 12, no. 4 (Autumn 2018): 37–44.

Bower, Bruce. "When It's Playtime, Many Kids Prefer Reality over Fantasy." *Science News*, February 6, 2018.

Brown, Tara Tiger. "The Death of Shop Class and America's Skilled Workforce." *Forbes*, May 20, 2012. forbes/com/sites/tarabrown/2012/05/30/the-death-of -shop-class-and-americas-high-skilled-workforce.

Deiss, Heather S., and Denise Miller. "Who Was Katherine Johnson?" *NASA Knows!* NASA, January 18, 2017, updated January 7, 2021.

Gigliotti, Jim. *Who Is Stevie Wonder?* New York: Grosset & Dunlap, 2016.

Green, Shulamite A., et al. "Overreactive Brain Responses to Sensory Stimuli in Youth with Autism Spectrum Disorders." *Journal of the American Academy of Child & Adolescent Psychiatry* 52, no. 11 (November 2013): 1158–1172.

Greene, Jay P., Brian Kisida, and Daniel H. Bowen. "Why Field Trips Matter." *Museum*, January 1, 2014. aam-us.org/2014/01/01/why-field-trips-matter.

Gross, Ashley, and Jon Marcus. "High-Paying Trade Jobs Sit Empty, While High School Grads Line Up for University." NPR, April 25, 2018. npr.org/sections /ed/2018/04/25/605092520/high-paying-trade-jobs-sit-empty-while-high-school -grads-line-up-for-university.

Hacker, Andrew. "Is Algebra Necessary?" *New York Times*, July 28, 2012. nytimes .com/2012/07/29/opinion/sunday/is-algebra-necessary.html.

Jaswal, Vikram K., Allison Wayne, and Hudson Golino. "Eye-Tracking Reveals

Agency in Assisted Autistic Communication." *Scientific Reports* 10 (May 2020): article no. 7882.

Jewish Virtual Library. "Nazi Euthanasia Program: Persecution of the Mentally and Physically Disabled." jewishvirtuallibrary.org/nazi-persecution-of-the-mentally -and-physically-disabled.

Keith, Jessica M., Jeremy P. Jamieson, and Loisa Bennetto. "The Influence of Noise on Autonomic Arousal and Cognitive Performance in Adolescents with Autism Spectrum Disorder." *Journal of Autism and Developmental Disorders* 49, no. 1 (January 2019): 113–126.

Louv, Richard. *Last Child in the Woods: Saving Our Children from Nature-Deficit Disorder.* Chapel Hill, NC: Algonquin Books, 2005.

Mukhopadhyay, Tito Rajarshi. *How Can I Talk If My Lips Don't Move: Inside My Autistic Mind.* New York: Arcade, 2011.

Root-Bernstein, Robert, et al. "Arts Foster Scientific Success: Avocations of Nobel, National Academy, Royal Society, and Sigma Xi Members." *Journal of Psychology of Science and Technology* 1, no. 2 (October 2008): 51–63.

Rosen, Julia. "How a Hobby Can Boost Researchers' Productivity and Creativity." *Nature* 558 (2018): 475–477.

Schoen, Sarah A., et al. "A Systematic Review of Ayres Sensory Integration Intervention for Children with Autism." *Autism Research* 12, no. 1 (January 2019): 6–19.

Taggart, Jessica, Megan J. Heise, and Angeline S. Lillard. "The Real Thing: Preschoolers Prefer Actual Activities to Pretend Ones." *Developmental Science* 21, no. 3 (May 2018). doi.org/10.1111/desc.12582.

Watanabe, Teresa, and Rosanna Xia. "Drop Algebra Requirements for Non-STEM Majors, California Community Colleges Chief Says." *Los Angeles Times*, July 17, 2017. latimes.com/local/lanow/la-me-california-community-colleges-algebra -20170717-story.html.

Winerip, Michael. "A Field Trip to a Strange New Place: Second Grade Visits the Parking Garage." *New York Times*, February 12, 2012. nytimes.com/2012/02/13 /nyregion/for-poorer-students-an-attempt-to-let-new-experiences-guide-learning .html.

Chapter Three: Clever Engineers

Burger, Dan, et al. "Filtergraph: A Flexible Web Application for Instant Data Visualization of Astronomy Datasets." Originally presented at the ADASS XXII Conference in Champaign, IL, on November 6, 2012. Published in the conference proceedings by ASP Conference Series. arXiv:1212:4458.

Ferguson, Eugene S. "The Mind's Eye: Nonverbal Thought in Technology." *Science* 197, no. 4306 (August 1977): 827–836.

Gold, Russell, Katherine Blunt, and Talal Ansari. "PG&E Reels as California Wildfire Burns." *Wall Street Journal*, October 26, 2019, A1–A2.

Gold, Russell, Renée Rigdon, and Yaryna Serkez. "PG&E's Network Heightens California's Fire Risk." *Wall Street Journal*, October 30, 2019, A6.

Jacobs, Julia. "Seven of the Deadliest Infrastructure Failures throughout History." *New York Times*, August 14, 2018. nytimes.com/2018/08/14/world/bridge -collapses-history.html.

Lewis, Randy. *No Greatness Without Goodness: How a Father's Love Changed a Company and Sparked a Movement*. Carol Stream, IL: Tyndale House, 2016.

"PSPS Wind Update: Wind Gusts in Nearly Two Dozen Counties Reached above 40 MPH; in 15 Counties Wind Gusts Topped 50 MPH." Business Wire, October 16, 2019. businesswire.comnews/home/2019016005951/en/PSPS-Wind-Update -Wing-Gusts-inNearly-Two-Dozen-Counties-Reached-Above-40-MPH-in-15 -Counties-Wind-Gusts-Topped-50-MPH.

Rubin, Shira. "The Israeli Army Unit That Recruits Teens with Autism." *Atlantic*, January 6, 2016. theatlantic.com/health/archive/2016/01/israeli -army-autism/422850/.

Sales, Ben. "Deciphering Satellite Photos, Soldiers with Autism Take on Key Roles in IDF." Jewish Telegraphic Agency, December 8, 2015. jta.org/2015/12/08/israel /deciphering-satellite-photos-soldiers-with-autism-take-on-key-roles-in-idf.

Schwartz, Nelson D. "A New Look at Apprenticeships as a Path to the Middle Class." *New York Times*, July 13, 2015.

Stockman, Farah. "Want a White-Collar Career without College Debt? Become an Apprentice." *New York Times*, December 10, 2019.

Chapter 4 : Complementary Minds

Chaikin, Andrew. "Neil Armstrong's Spacesuit Was Made by Bra Manufacturer." *Smithsonian Magazine*, November 2013. smithsonianmag.com/history/neil -armstrongs-spacesuit-was-made-by-a-bra-manfacturer-3652414.

Davis, Allison P. "The Epic Battle behind the Apollo Spacesuit." *Wired*, February 28, 2011. wired.com/2011/02/pl-spacesuits-showdown.

de Monchaux, Nicholas. *Spacesuit: Fashioning Apollo*. Cambridge, MA: MIT Press, 2011.

Fishman, Charles. "The Improbable Story of the Bra-Maker Who Won the Right to Make Astronaut Spacesuits." *Fast Company*, July 15, 2019. fastcompany .com/90375440/the-improbable-story-of-the-bra-maker-who-won-the-right -to-make-astronaut-spacesuits.

Fuller, Thomas. "Underdog No More, a Deaf Football Team Takes California by Storm." *New York Times*, November 15, 2021. nytimes.com/2021/11/15 /us/riverside-california-deaf-football-team.html.

Grandin, Temple. "Double Rail Restrainer Conveyor for Livestock Handling."
Journal of Agricultural Engineering Research 41, no. 4 (December 1988):
327–338.

Hines, William C., et al. "Sorting Out the FACS: A Devil in the Details." *Cell Reports*
6, no. 5 (March 2014): 779–781.

Isaacson, Walter. *Steve Jobs*. New York: Simon & Schuster, 2011.

Jobs, Steve. "You've Got to Find What You Love." Commencement Address, Stanford
University. *Stanford News*, June 12, 2005.

Kuang, Cliff. "The 6 Pillars of Steve Jobs's Design Philosophy." *Fast Company*,
November 7, 2011. fastcompany.com/1665375/the-6-pillars-of-steve-jobss
-design-philosophy.

Nolan, Frederick. *The Sound of Their Music: The Story of Rodgers & Hammerstein*.
New York: Applause Theatre & Cinema Books, 2002.

Purves, John C., and Lennox F. Beach. Magnetic Field Responsive Device. US Patent
2383460A, issued 1945.

Reynolds, Alison, and David Lewis. "Teams Solve Problems Faster When They're
More Cognitively Diverse." *Harvard Business Review*, March 30, 2017.
hbr.org/2017/03/teams-solve-problems-faster-when-theyre-more-cognitively
-diverse.

Rogers, Taylor Nicole. "Meet Eric Yuan, the Founder and CEO of Zoom, Who Has
Made Over $12 Billion Since March and Now Ranks among the 400 Richest
People in America." *Business Insider*, September 9, 2020. businessinsider.com
/meet-zoom-billionaire-eric-yuan-career-net-worth-life.

Schindler, Janine. "The Benefits of Cognitive Diversity." *Forbes*, November 26, 2018.
forbes.com/sites/forbescoachescouncil/2018/11/26/the-benefits-of-cognitive
-diversity.

"The Seamstresses Who Helped Put Men on the Moon." CBS News, July 14, 2019.

cbsnews.com/news/apollo-11-the-seamstresses-who-helped-put-a-man-on-the
-moon.

Wattles, Jackie. "She Turns Elon Musk's Bold Space Ideas into a Business." CNN
Business, March 10, 2019. cnn.com/2019/03/10/tech/spacex-coo-gwynne
-shotwell-profile/index.html.

Wozniak, Steve, with Gina Smith. *iWOZ: Computer Geek to Cult Icon: How I
Invented the Personal Computer, Co-Founded Apple, and Had Fun Doing It.*
New York: W.W. Norton, 2006.

Chapter Five: Defining Genius

Blumenthal, Karen. *Steve Jobs: The Man Who Thought Different.* New York: Feiwel
and Friends, 2012.

Bouchard, Thomas J., Jr., et al. "Sources of Human Psychological Differences: The
Minnesota Study of Twins Reared Apart." *Science* 250, no. 4978 (October 1990):
223–228.

Carrillo-Mora, Paul, et al. "What Did Einstein Have That I Don't? Studies on Albert
Einstein's Brain." *Neurosciences and History* 3, no. 3 (2015): 125–129.

Falk, Dean. "New Information about Albert Einstein's Brain." *Frontiers in
Evolutionary Neuroscience* 1 (May 2009). doi.org/10.3389/neuro.18.003.2009.

Felicetti, Kristen. "These Major Tech Companies Are Making Autism Hiring a
Priority." *Fortune*, March 8, 2016.

Foster, Brian. "Einstein and His Love of Music." *Physics World* 18, no. 1 (2005): 34.

Gable, Shelly L., Elizabeth A. Hopper, and Jonathan W. Schooler. "When the Muses
Strike: Creative Ideas of Physicists and Writers Routinely Occur during Mind
Wandering." *Psychological Science* 30, no. 3 (March 2019): 396–404.

"The Girl Who Asked Questions." *Economist*, February 29, 2020, 72.

Haskell, Molly. *Steven Spielberg: A Life in Films*. New Haven: Yale University Press, 2017.

Hodges, Andrew. *Alan Turing: The Enigma*. Princeton, NJ: Princeton University Press, 2014.

Isaacson, Walter. *Einstein: His Life and Universe*. New York: Simon & Schuster, 2007.

Kapoula, Zoï, and Marine Vernet. "Dyslexia, Education and Creativity, a Cross-Cultural Study." *Aesthetics and Neuroscience* (December 2016): 31–42.

McFarland, Matt. "Why Shades of Asperger's Syndrome Are the Secret to Building a Great Tech Company." *Washington Post*, April 3, 2015. washingtonpost.com /news/innovations/wp/2015/04/03/why-shades-of-aspergers-syndrome-are-the -secret-to-building-a-great-tech-company.

Miller, Greg. "Music Builds Bridges in the Brain." *Science*, April 16, 2008.

Patten, Bernard M. "Visually Mediated Thinking: A Report of the Case of Albert Einstein." *Journal of Learning Disabilities* 6, no. 7 (October 1973). doi .org/10.1177/002221947300600702.

Reser, Jared Edward. "Solitary Mammals Provide an Animal Model for Autism Spectrum Disorders." *Journal of Comparative Psychology* 128, no. 1 (2014): 99–113.

Sacks, Oliver. *An Anthropologist on Mars: Seven Paradoxical Tales*. New York: Alfred A. Knopf, 1995.

Seabrook, John. "E-Mail from Bill." *New Yorker*, January 10, 1994.

"Steven Spielberg Escaped His Dyslexia through Filmmaking." ABC News, September 27, 2012. abcnews.go.com/blogs/entertainment/2012/09/steven-spielberg -escaped-his-dyslexia-through-filmmaking.

Than, Ker. "A Brief History of Twin Studies." *Smithsonian Magazine*, March 4, 2016. smithsonianmag.com/science-nature/brief-history-twin-studies-180958281.

West, Thomas G. *In the Mind's Eye: Creative Visual Thinkers, Gifted Dyslexics, and the*

Rise of Visual Technologies. 2nd edition. Amherst, NY: Prometheus Books, 2009.

Wolff, Ulrika, and Ingvar Lundberg. "The Prevalence of Dyslexia among Art Students." *Dyslexia* 8, no. 1 (January–March 2002): 34–42. doi.org/10.1002/dys.211.

Chapter Six: Visualizing Disaster

Baker, Mike, and Dominic Gates. "Lack of Redundancies on Boeing 737 MAX System Baffles Some Involved in Developing the Jet." *Seattle Times*, March 26, 2019. seattletimes.com/business/boeing-aerospace/a-lack-of-redundancies-on-737-max-system-has-baffled-even-those-who-worked-on-the-jet.

Davis, Carolyn. "Merrimack Valley Gas Pipeline Contractors Lacked Necessary Replacement Info, Says NTSB." National Gas Intelligence, October 12, 2018. naturalgasintel.com/merrimack-valley-gas-pipeline-contractors-lacked-necessary-replacement-info-says-ntsb.

Federal Aviation Administration. Air Worthiness Directives; Transport and Commuter Category Airplanes. Docket No. FAA-2021-0953. Project Identifier AD-2021-01169-T.

Ford, Dana. "Cheney's Defibrillator Was Modified to Prevent Hacking." CNN, October 24, 2013. cnn.com/2013/10/20/us/dick-cheney-gupta-interview/index.html.

Gates, Dominic, and Mike Baker. "The Inside Story of MCAS: How Boeing's 737 MAX System Gained Power and Lost Safeguards." *Seattle Times*, June 22, 2019. seattletimes.com/seattle-news/times-watchdog/the-inside-story-of-mcas-how-boeings-737-max-system-gained-power-and-lost-safeguards.

Gibson, Eleanor J., and Richard D. Walk. "The 'Visual Cliff.'" *Scientific American* 202, no. 4 (April 1960): 64–71.

Glanz, James, et al. "Jet's Software Was Updated, Pilots Weren't." *New York Times*, February 3, 2019, 1, 18.

Gulati, Ranjay, Charles Casto, and Charlotte Krontiris. "How the Other Fukushima

Plant Survived." *Harvard Business Review*, July–August 2014. hbr.org/2014/07 /how-the-other-fukushima-plant-survived.

Herkert, Joseph, Jason Borenstein, and Keith Miller. "The Boeing 737 MAX: Lessons for Engineering Ethics." *Science and Engineering Ethics* 26 (December 2020): 2957–2974.

Kaiser, Jocelyn. "Key Cancer Results Failed to be Reproduced." *Science* 374, no. 6573 (December 2021): 1311.

Mullard, Asher. "Half of Top Cancer Studies Fail High-Profile Reproducibility Effort." *Nature*, December 9, 2021. nature.com/articles/d41586-021-03691-0.

Peterson, Andrea. "Yes, Terrorists Could Have Hacked Dick Cheney's Heart." *Washington Post*, October 21, 2013. washingtonpost.com/news/the-switch /wp/2013/10/21/yes-terrorists-could-have-hacked-dick-cheneys-heart.

Phillips, Michael, et al. "Detection of Malignant Melanoma Using Artificial Intelligence: An Observational Study of Diagnostic Accuracy." *Dermatology Practical and Conceptual* 10, no. 1 (January 2020): e202011.

Silver, David, et al. "Mastering the Game of GO without Human Knowledge." *Nature* 550 (October 2017): 354–359.

Sullenberger, Captain "Sully." "Letter to the Editor" in "What Really Brought Down the Boeing 737 Max?" *New York Times Magazine*, October 13, 2019, 16.

Tung, Stephen. "The Day the Golden Gate Bridge Flattened." *Mercury News*, May 23, 2012. mercurynews.com/2012/05/23/the-day-the-golden-gate-bridge-flattened.

US Nuclear Regulatory Commission. "Backgrounder on the Three Mile Island Accident." Updated November 15, 2022. nrc.gov/reading-rm/doc-collections/fact -sheets/3mile-isle.html.

Washington State Department of Transportation. "Tacoma Narrows Bridge History— Lessons from the Failure of a Great Machine." wsdot.wa.gov/tnbhistory /bridges-failure.htm#:~:text=Farquharson%20continued%20wind%20 tunnel%20tests,caused%20the%20bridge%20to%20fail.

Weinstein, Dave. "Hackers May Be Coming for Your City's Water Supply." *Wall Street Journal*, February 26, 2021. wsj.com/articles/hackers-may-be-coming-for -your-citys-water-supply-11614379990.

Chapter Seven: Animal Thinking

ASPCA. "History of the ASPCA." American Society for the Protection of Animals, 2020. aspca.org/about-us/history-of-the-ASPCA.

Bailey, Ida E., et al. "Image Analysis of Weaverbird Nests Reveals Signature Weave Textures." *Royal Society Open Science* 2, no. 6 (June 2015). doi.org/10.1098 /rsos.150074.

Bates, Mary. "Bumble Bees Can Recognize Objects Across Senses." *Psychology Today*, February 20, 2020. psychologytoday.com/us/blog/animal-minds/202002 /bumble-bees-can-recognize-objects-across-senses.

Berns, Gregory. *What It's Like to be a Dog: And Other Adventures in Animal Neuro- science*. New York: Basic Books, 2017.

Betz, Eric. "A Brief History of Chimps in Space." *Discover*, April 21, 2020. discovermagazine.com/the-sciences/a-brief-history-of-chimps-in-space.

Birch, Jonathan, Alexandra K. Schnell, and Nicola S. Clayton. "Dimensions of Animal Consciousness." *Trends in Cognitive Sciences* 24, no. 10 (October 2020): 789–801.

Borrell, Brendan. "Are Octopuses Smart?" *Scientific American*, February 27, 2009. scientificamerican.com/article/are-octopuses-smart.

Breland, Keller, and Marian Breland. "The Misbehavior of Organisms." *American Psychologist* 16, no. 11 (1961): 681–684.

Ceurstemont, Sandrine. "Inside a Wasp's Head: Here's What It Sees to Find Its Way Home." *New Scientist*, February 12, 2016. newscientist.com/article/2077306 -inside-a-wasps-head-heres-what-it-sees-to-find-its-way-home.

"Charles Henry Turner." Biogaphy.com, April 2, 2014, updated September 3, 2020. biography.com/scientists/charles-henry-turner.

Cook, Peter, et al. "Jealousy in Dogs? Evidence from Brain Imaging." *Animal Sentience* 22, no. 1 (2018). doi.org/10.51291/2377-7478.1319.

Dagg, Anne Innis. *Giraffe: Biology, Behaviour and Conservation.* New York: Cambridge University Press, 2014.

Davis, Kenneth L., and Christian Montag. "Selected Principles of Pankseppian Affective Neuroscience." *Frontiers in Neuroscience* 12 (January 2019): article no. 1025. doi.org/10.3389 /fnins.2018.01025.

Douglas-Hamilton, Iain, et al. "Behavioural Reactions of Elephants Towards a Dying and Deceased Matriarch." *Applied Animal Behaviour Science* 100, no. 1–2 (October 2006): 87–102. doi.org/10.1016/j.applanim.2006.04.014.

Favre, David, and Vivien Tsang. "The Development of the Anti-Cruelty Laws During the 1800s." *Detroit College of Law Review* 1 (1993).

Foster, Craig. *My Octopus Teacher.* Directed by Pippa Ehrlich and James Reed, Netflix, 2020.

Goodall, Jane. "Tool-Using and Aimed Throwing in a Community of Free-Living Chimpanzees." *Nature* 201 (March 1964): 1264–1266.

Grandin, Temple. *Temple Grandin's Guide to Working with Farm Animals: Safe, Humane Livestock Handling Practices for the Small Farm.* North Adams, MA: Storey Publishing, 2017.

Grandin, Temple, and Catherine Johnson. *Animals in Translation: Using the Mysteries of Autism to Decode Animal Behavior.* New York: Scribner, 2005.

Gray, Tara. "A Brief History of Animals in Space." NASA, 1998, updated April 3, 2014. history.nasa.gov/animals.html.

Herculano-Houzel, Susana. "Numbers of Neurons as Biological Correlates of

Cognitive Capability." *Current Opinion in Behavioral Sciences* 16 (August 2017): 1–7.

Hunt, Gavin R. "Manufacture and Use of Hook-Tools by New Caledonian Crows." *Nature* 379 (January 1996): 249–251.

Jacobs, Lucia F., and Emily R. Liman. "Grey Squirrels Remember the Locations of Buried Nuts." *Animal Behavior* 41, no. 1 (January 1991): 103–110.

Knight, Kathryn. "Paper Wasps Really Recognise Each Other's Faces." *Journal of Experimental Biology* 220, no. 12 (June 2017): 2129. doi.org/10.1242/jeb.163477.

Koch, Christof. "What Is Consciousness?: Scientists Are Beginning to Unravel a Mystery That Has Long Vexed Philosophers." *Nature* 557 (2018): S8–S12. doi.org/10.1038/d41586-018-05097-x.

Morris, C.L., Temple Grandin, and Nancy A. Irlbeck. "Companion Animals Symposium: Environmental Enrichment for Companion, Exotic, and Laboratory Animals." *Journal of Animal Science* 89, no. 12 (December 2011): 4227–4238.

Olkowicz, Seweryn, et al. "Birds Have Primate-Like Numbers of Neurons in the Forebrain." *Proceedings of the National Academy of Sciences* 113, no. 26 (June 2016): 7255–7260. doi.org/10.1073/pnas.1517131113.

Panksepp, Jaak. "The Basic Emotional Circuits of Mammalian Brains: Do Animals Have Affective Lives?" *Neuroscience and Biobehavioral Reviews* 35, no. 9 (October 2011): 1791–1804.

Plotnik, Joshua M., Frans B. M. de Waal, and Diana Reiss. "Self-Recognition in an Asian Elephant." *Proceedings of the National Academy of Sciences* 103, no. 45 (November 2006): 17053–17057.

Prior, Helmut, Ariane Schwarz, and Onur Güntürkün. "Mirror-Induced Behavior in the Magpie (Pica pica): Evidence of Self-Recognition." *PLOS Biology* 6, no, 8 (August 2008): e202. doi.org/10.1371/journal.pbio.0060202.

Raby, C.R., et al. "Planning for the Future by Western Scrub-Jays." *Nature* 445 (February 2007): 919–921.

Reiss, Diana. *The Dolphin in the Mirror: Exploring Dolphin Minds and Saving Dolphin Lives.* New York: Houghton Mifflin Harcourt, 2011.

Skinner, B. F. "Why I Am Not a Cognitive Psychologist." *Behaviorism* 5, no. 2 (Fall 1977): 1–10.

Solvi, Cwyn, Selene Gutierrez Al-Khudhairy, and Lars Chittka. "Bumble Bees Display Cross-Modal Object Recognition Between Visual and Tactile Senses." *Science* 367, no. 6480 (February 2020): 910–912.

Stacho, Martin, et al. "A Cortex-Like Canonical Circuit in the Avian Forebrain." *Science* 369, no. 6511 (September 2020). doi.10.1126/science.abc5534.

von Bayern, A. M. P., et al. "Compound Tool Construction by New Caledonian Crows." *Scientific Reports* 8 (October 2018): article no. 15676.

Watanabe, Shigeru, Junko Sakamoto, and Masumi Wakita. "Pigeons' Discrimination of Paintings by Monet and Picasso." *Journal of the Experimental Analysis of Behavior* 63, no, 2 (March 1995): 165–174.

Image Credits

Page 6, Courtesy of the author

Page 13, Courtesy of the author

Page 17, (left) Courtesy of Norbert Levajsics via Unsplash, (right) Courtesy of Mack Male via Wikimedia Commons

Page 22, Courtesy of Wikimedia Commons

Page 23, Courtesy of Anatomy & Physiology, Connexions Web site. http://cnx.org /content/col11496/1.6/, Jun 19, 2013, via Wikimedia Commons. Components of this image were created by the publisher.

Page 29, Courtesy of the author

Page 30, Courtesy of the author

Page 36, Courtesy of Haltopub via Wikimedia Commons

Page 41, Courtesy of Southwarth and Hawes via Wikimedia Commons

Page 42, Courtesy of the Smithsonian

Page 51, Courtesy of the 1968 Michiganensian, p. 91, via Wikimedia Commons

Page 52, Courtesy of Waterlily16 via Wikimedia Commons

Page 53, Courtesy of the author

Page 55, Courtesy of NASA

Page 66, Courtesy of ESA/Hubble & NASA, F. Pacaud, D. Coe

Page 67, Courtesy of the author

Page 68, Courtesy of the author

Page 69, Courtesy of the author

Page 72, Courtesy of vlasta2 via Wikimedia Commons

Page 73, Courtesy of Leading American Inventors by George Iles (1912), p. 300, via Wikimedia Commons

Page 77, Courtesy of NASA/JPL-Caltech/MSSS

Page 79, (left and right) Courtesy of the author

Page 96, Courtesy of the United States Patent and Trademark Office

Page 105, Courtesy of Philafrenzy via Wikimedia Commons

Page 108, Courtesy of Bernard Gotfryd via the United States Library of Congress

Page 111, Courtesy of Wikimedia Commons

Page 115, Courtesy of NASA

Page 119, Courtesy of Gallica: Les Merveilles de l'Aviation/Branger via Wikimedia Commons

Page 124, (top) Courtesy of René Mayorga via Wikimedia Commons, (bottom) Courtesy of Gregory "Slobirdr" Smith via Wikimedia Commons

Page 130, Courtesy of William A. Macis via Wikimedia Commons

Page 135, Courtesy of Alessandro Nassiri via Wikimedia Commons

Page 142, Courtesy of the author

Page 144, Courtesy of Gibson and Walk (1960) via Wikimedia Commons

Page 152, Courtesy of Wikimedia Commons

Page 158, Courtesy of Hannes Grobe via Wikimedia Commons

Page 167, Courtesy of Kawamoto Takuo via Wikimedia Commons

Pages 174, Courtesy of Grafiker61 via Wikimedia Commons

Page 179, (left) Courtesy of via Wikimedia Commons, (right) Courtesy of Gérard Edelinck and Frans Hals/Gallica Digital Library via Wikimedia Commons

Page 182, Courtesy of the British Library

Page 188, Courtesy of Livefornature via Wikimedia Commons

Page 189, Courtesy of Bernard DUPONT via Wikimedia Commons

Page 191, Courtesy of AndreasJS via Wikimedia Commons

Page 196, Courtesy of Georgia Pinaud via Wikimedia Commons

Page 198, Courtesy of NASA

Page 199, Courtesy of NobelPrize.org via Wikimedia Commons

Page 203, Courtesy of Gregory Berns